Interpreting
the Bible

Elements of Preaching
O. Wesley Allen Jr., series editor

Thinking Theologically
The Preacher as Theologian
Ronald J. Allen

Knowing the Context
Frames, Tools, and Signs for Preaching
James R. Nieman

Interpreting the Bible
Approaching the Text in Preparation for Preaching
Mary F. Foskett

Shaping the Claim
Moving from Text to Sermon
Marvin A. McMickle

Determining the Form
Structures for Preaching
O. Wesley Allen Jr.

Finding Language and Imagery
Words for Holy Speech
Jennifer L. Lord

Delivering the Sermon
Voice, Body, and Animation in Proclamation
Teresa L. Fry Brown

Serving the Word
Preaching in Worship
Melinda A. Quivik

Interpreting the Bible

Approaching the Text in Preparation for Preaching

Mary F. Foskett

Fortress Press
Minneapolis

INTERPRETING THE BIBLE
Approaching the Text in Preparation for Preaching

Cover image: © iStockphoto.com/Igor Skrynnikov
Cover and book design: John Goodman

Library of Congress Cataloging-in-Publication Data
Foskett, Mary F., 1961–
  Interpreting the Bible : approaching the text in preparation for preaching / Mary F. Foskett.
    p. cm. — (Elements of preaching)
  Includes bibliographical references.
  ISBN 978-0-8006-6354-4 (alk. paper)
  1. Bible—Hermeneutics. 2. Bible—Homiletical use. 3. Bible—Criticism, interpretation, etc.
  4. Preaching. I. Title.
  BS476.F66 2009
  220.601—dc22
                              2009012030

Contents

Editor's Foreword

Preparing beginning preachers to stand before the body of Christ and proclaim the word of God faithfully, authentically, and effectively Sunday after Sunday is and always has been a daunting responsibility. As North American pastors face pews filled with citizens of a postmodern, post-Christendom culture, this teaching task becomes even more complex. The theological, exegetical, and homiletical skills that preachers need for the future are as much in flux today as they have ever been in Western Christianity. Thus providing seminary students with a solid but flexible homiletical foundation at the start of their careers is a necessity.

Traditionally, professors of preaching choose a primary introductory textbook that presents a theology of proclamation and a process of sermon development and delivery from a single point of view. To maintain such a singular point of view is the sign of good writing, but it does at times cause problems for learning in pluralistic settings. One approach to preaching does not fit all. Yet a course simply surveying all of the homiletical possibilities available will not provide a foundation on which to build either.

Furthermore, while there are numerous introductory preaching textbooks from which to choose, most are written from the perspective of Euro-American males. Classes supplement this view with smaller homiletical texts written by women and persons of color. But a pedagogical hierarchy is nevertheless set up: the white male voice provides the main course and women and persons of color provide the side dishes.

Elements of Preaching is a series designed to help professors and students of preaching—including established preachers who want to develop their skills in specific areas—construct a sound homiletical foundation in a conversational manner. This conversation is meant to occur at two levels. First, the series as a whole deals with basic components found in most introductory preaching classes: theology of proclamation, homiletical contexts, biblical interpretation, sermonic claim, language and imagery, rhetorical form, delivery, and worship.

But each element is presented by a different scholar, all of whom represent diversity in terms of gender, theological traditions (Baptist, Disciple of Christ, Lutheran, Presbyterian, and United Methodist), and ethnicity (African American, Asian American, and Euro-American). Instead of bringing in different voices at the margin of the preaching class, Elements of Preaching creates a conversation around the central topics of an introductory course without foregoing essential instruction concerning sermon construction and embodiment. Indeed, this level of conversation is extended beyond the printed volumes through the Web site www.ElementsofPreaching.com.

Second, the individual volumes are written in an open-ended manner. The individual author's particular views are offered but in a way that invites, indeed demands, the readers to move beyond them in developing their own approaches to the preaching task. The volumes offer theoretical and practical insights, but at the last page it is clear that more must be said. Professors and students have a solid place to begin, but there is flexibility within the class (and after the class in ministry) to move beyond these volumes by building on the insights and advice they offer.

In this volume, Mary F. Foskett introduces readers to the essential elements of interpreting the biblical text for the sermon. Foskett walks a tightrope in offering preachers the main ingredients and broad methods of exegesis without offering a single recipe meant to create the one right dish. While Foskett shows preachers how to engage a text in order to discover a message for the pulpit, she refuses to allow a text to be reduced to that single message. Instead, preachers are invited to explore what they find *in* the text (the literary, theological qualities of the passage), *behind* the text (the historical context[s] of the passage), and *before* the text (the context of the contemporary community from which and to which we preach). Foskett invites the readers, as they begin to make the move from the text to the pulpit, to consider how these different arenas of exploration relate to one another and how to struggle with a passage that is troubling. Preachers who listen to biblical texts in the ways Foskett suggests will find themselves rich in new ways. They will no longer ask in anguish, "*What* can I preach from this text?" Instead, in joy, they will, "*Which* of the meanings I have discovered through this process of reading will I offer to my congregation this week?"

O. Wesley Allen Jr.

Acknowledgments

I want to give special thanks to my editor, O. Wesley Allen, for his tremendous support while I worked on this book. Whereas the faults of the book are surely mine, Wes's keen eye and sharp editorial skills made the results of my efforts much better than they would otherwise have been. Thanks, Wes.

I also wish to thank David Lott at Fortress Press for his fine editing and his graciousness in working alongside me and Wes to bring this project to its successful completion.

Finally, I thank my husband, Scott, and our wonderful son, Daniel, for their good patience and constant support while I worked on this volume. It is to them that I dedicate this book.

Introduction

Before the Sermon
Interpreting the Biblical Text

What I now understand to be among the most important lessons of my seminary education occurred during my very first semester as an M.Div. student. Having entered seminary with a primary interest in pastoral care, I enrolled in my first foundational course in biblical studies with the intention of meeting a core requirement and then quickly moving on to what really interested me. Little did I know that I was about to be ushered into what would eventually become the center of my life's work. Nor did I realize that biblical studies had to do not only with the collection of sacred texts that we call the Bible, but also with the communities of faith who read Scripture and the lives of individual readers. In that first semester of my seminary education, my life was forever changed by the revelation, one that has deepened in the years since, that biblical interpretation is not a simply a by-product of careful study and research. Rather, the interpretation of Scripture is a dynamic process that is shaped in important ways by the readers who engage and relate to the text. Biblical interpretation has as much to do with real people and real-world concerns as with the biblical texts that we interpret. It has as much to do with our lives in real time as with those of the great cloud of witnesses whose stories and contexts the Bible tells and reveals. Nowhere is this concept more important than in the interpretation of the Bible for sermon preparation. For, at its best, the sermon proclaims God's living word in a way that enlivens both the biblical text and the community of faith.

In the spirit of what I began to understand first as a seminary student and have continued to examine since, this book is written primarily for M.Div. students and clergypersons seeking a concise introduction to current practices of critical biblical interpretation for sermon preparation as well as focused discussion of key facets of the interpretive process. It is not intended to replace the excellent introductions to biblical exegesis that have been previously published nor does it claim to provide a comprehensive discussion of the many methods that have been or are currently utilized in the field of biblical studies. Rather, this book aims to provide a framework for approaching the Bible that will deepen and broaden preachers' understanding of both the complexity and accessibility of biblical interpretation. It is, at its heart, an invitation to enter into deeper relationship with the Scripture that readers seek to understand, interpret, and preach both critically and faithfully.

What Is Exegesis?

There are many ways to read and study Scripture. No single approach to biblical interpretation can define how anyone, even a person of faith, should read the Bible. As a critical discipline, biblical studies offers readers particular frameworks, as well as specific tools, for engaging the biblical text. The field of biblical studies uses the term *exegesis* to describe the task of interpreting the Bible. Exegesis is often upheld in contrast to *eisegeis*. A classic formulation that distinguishes exegesis (from the Greek, "to lead out") from eisegesis ("to lead in") argues that whereas eisegesis entails reading into a text in such a way that imposes external ideas and meaning onto it, exegesis seeks to interpret a text by analyzing the language and content of the text itself. Proponents of exegesis also tend to assume that proper examination of the biblical text will yield the single most correct interpretation of the passage. We will see that to the extent that every reader brings a particular set of values, expectations, and questions to the Bible, some eisegesis is unavoidable and a plurality of plausible interpretations is always possible. What sets exegesis apart from pure eisegesis is its careful attention to the process of reading and interpreting the Bible and its respect for the text's complexity.

Perhaps a second contrast between two ways of reading the Bible will also prove illustrative. In the current revival of contemplative prayer, laypersons and clergy alike are increasingly taking up the ancient meditative practice of *lectio divina* as a means of praying the Scriptures. If we conceive of *lectio divina* as a practice of spiritual formation of an individual or small group, we may think of exegesis as a practice of critical formation wherein readers examine various aspects of the biblical text, including its historical dimensions and its interpretation and appropriation by religious communities. To consider intentionally the historical aspect of the Bible is to understand the Bible as thoroughly "anthropological."[1] As New Testament scholar Luke Timothy Johnson suggests, "[T]he writings must be taken seriously as fully *human* productions. Divine inspiration is not excluded, but inspiration is not a fact available for study."[2] To acknowledge the Bible as a human production is to understand that its contents were written and its transmission carried out by human persons living in a particular time in real places. It is also to take seriously the notion that as readers, we hear, see, engage, and respond to the Bible in particular ways that conform or respond to the contours of our own time, history, and place in the world. In other words, the Bible is a collection of texts that were written and were subsequently read and interpreted, and continue to be interpreted, by real men and women of faith living in particular places at specific times in human history and with very real concerns. In attending to the historical aspects of Scripture, especially in light of the composition, transmission, and appropriation of its various texts, exegesis seeks to arrive at an understanding of what a biblical text may be saying to contemporary readers, what the text means for today, and how it is that we can arrive at such meaning in the first place.

Readers new to critical interpretation of the Bible, especially preaching students and clergy who have been studying (and perhaps even preaching from) the Bible for years, may indeed be wondering what all the fuss is about. Why can't readers simply read the text and immediately move to preparing the sermon? Of course, readers can choose to read and write their sermons this way. However, it is important to recognize that the call for careful exegesis arises from the nature of the biblical texts themselves. As Johnson writes of biblical interpretation, or hermeneutics:

Now, if Scripture spoke uniformly and clearly on every subject, if its commands and directives were entirely consistent, if all its compositions represented precisely the same perspective on identical issues, then the only real hermeneutical problem would be that of translating both its words and the situations it address to present circumstances—not a small task, to be sure, but not an impossible one, either. Scripture, however, does not speak in so straightforward a fashion. Besides speaking in ancient languages only partly grasped by contemporary readers and addressing situations mostly obscure to them, Scripture presents an almost bewildering variety of perspectives among its compositions and reveals in its directives, inconsistencies, and even contradictions on a significant number of issues. Finally, Scripture simply does not speak either clearly or directly to any number of issues that are important to its present-day readers.[3]

A collection of varied and ancient texts, the Bible is neither simple nor does it speak with only one voice and from one moment in time and space. That Christian readers uphold these texts as sacred and authoritative is only the starting point for the person who is preparing to preach. The hard work comes in interpreting these texts, discerning the word to preach, and crafting the sermon.

For preachers who may be concerned that a methodical approach to interpreting the Bible might exclude the possibility of any formational engagement with Scripture, rest assured that exegesis should not hinder the process of moving from text to sermon nor exclude devotional reading of the text. What careful exegesis can do is illumine the text and the preacher's experience of it for the enrichment of preaching and the sake of his or her congregation. The aim of critical biblical interpretation for preaching is not to make reading the Bible unnecessarily complex. Rather, *the purpose of exegesis is to bring the complexity, richness, and power of the biblical text alive in such a way that enhances the faithful preaching of the divine, living word.*

Over the last fifty years, the field of biblical studies has witnessed a proliferation of methodologies and areas of specialization. Such expansion has been due to multiple factors, including, but not limited to, the discovery of the Dead Sea Scrolls and the Nag Hammadi library in the mid-twentieth century and the increasing interdisciplinarity of biblical studies. Over the past forty years, literary, feminist, and cultural studies as well as the social sciences have come to play an increasing role in biblical studies. Areas of specialization within biblical exegesis alone now include narrative, reader-response, rhetorical, feminist, ideological, postcolonial, postmodern, anthropological, and social-scientific methods of interpretation. Despite the methodological expansion of biblical studies over the years, one need not specialize in any of these methods in order to exegete responsibly a biblical passage for sermon preparation. What preachers will likely find more valuable is becoming familiar with the kinds of questions and avenues of inquiry that have emerged in this growing constellation of approaches to biblical interpretation. Doing so will allow preaching students and clergy to discern the usefulness and relevance of various kinds of questions and ways of studying the Bible each time they meditate upon a text in preparation for a sermon. With that said, this volume invites readers to think of biblical exegesis as a means of engaging the text with greater clarity, intimacy, and attention by becoming familiar with the multiple dimensions of Scripture and the ways in which readers might approach them.

The Three Worlds of the Bible

A helpful and often-used model for approaching biblical interpretation focuses readers' attention on three dimensions, or "three worlds," of the Bible.[4] This model is especially useful both for distinguishing the different aspects of the biblical text that readers engage and clarifying the kinds of questions and concerns that readers bring to their study of the Bible. Knowing both the nature of one's questions and the multidimensional nature of Scripture is essential to clear exegesis. It is also an important means toward engaging in dialogue with others about the interpretation of biblical texts. One reason why Christians too often find themselves caught up in vehement and fruitless arguments with one another about the interpretation of particular texts is because readers too seldom reflect either on the perspectives they bring to their reading of Scripture or the specific dimensions of the Bible with which their questions are concerned. Being more conscious and intentional about biblical interpretation makes it easier to engage others in meaningful conversation, even, or perhaps especially, if such discussion focuses on significant differences in interpretation. Finally, the "three worlds" model is useful for understanding the aims and concerns of the differing approaches to biblical exegesis that have evolved over the past forty years.

The three worlds of the Bible is a heuristic concept that corresponds to three areas of exegetical inquiry and study. Though they do not really exist in isolation from one another, focusing attention on one particular arena of inquiry at a time goes a long way toward facilitating a preacher and congregation's engagement with a biblical passage with greater care, precision, and intentionality. In subsequent chapters, readers will be invited to explore each of these three so-called worlds of the Bible: the *literary* world (the "world of the text"); the *historical* world (the "world behind the text"), and the *contemporary* world (the "world in front of the text"). What follows here is a brief description of each.

The Literary World

The literary world *of* the text concerns the information that can be gleaned from reading the biblical passage itself, without consulting resources beyond the Bible. When concentrating on the literary world of the text, one can determine the basic form of a text (for example, Is it a story or part of a story? A hymn? A letter or part of a letter?), its component parts (its beginning, middle, end) and elements (such as plot, setting, argument, point of view, characters, conflict, resolution, themes, repetition of words and ideas), as well as its relationship to the rest of the biblical book in which the passage is located (Does it occur in the beginning, middle, or end of the biblical book? How does the passage relate to what precedes and what follows? How does it function in the book's entire story or argument or structure? Does it contain themes or motifs that occur elsewhere in the book?). Many scholars refer to this process as a "close reading" of the text. To read a biblical passage in this way is to give careful attention to its rhetorical and literary contours as well as its larger literary context. It acknowledges that the Bible is a collection of literatures, discourses, and texts. It also understands that respecting and examining the literary dimensions of the Bible will help bring it even more to life for the reader.

The Historical World

The historical world of the Bible, or the world *behind* the text, is an equally important area of inquiry that pertains to several aspects of the text. As the designation suggests, this dimension of biblical literature gives special attention to the historical nature of the Bible. As a collection of sacred texts, the Bible was written and edited, and later transmitted and interpreted, in particular and quite varied historical contexts. When studying the Bible, readers often engage different historical aspects of the Bible at the same time. Cultivating a greater awareness of the historical world of the Bible lends additional clarity and integrity to a reader's exegesis.

The historical world of the Bible consists of the following: the historical context to which a biblical text refers; the historical context in which a biblical text was composed; the history of a text's composition, redaction (editing), and transmission; the history of a text's translation; and the history of a text's interpretation and appropriation (including its eventual inclusion in the canon). A question that may immediately come to mind is, "What difference does it make whether or not one pays attention to the historical context of the story or its composition?" If the difference between these contexts is not initially apparent, let us consider for a moment another piece of literature, specifically an example from English literature: William Shakespeare's play, *Julius Caesar*. The historical context to which the story refers is that of ancient Rome in the first century B.C.E. While we can determine the general setting of the play from a close reading of the text, familiarity with the historical world and events to which the play refers helps readers fill out their understanding of the main characters as well as the circumstances and conflicts that shape their relationships to one another. Yet as relevant as it may be, consideration of the world to which *Julius Caesar* refers does not fully account for the play's historical dimensions. Shakespeare's own historical context, too, lends shape to his play. The concerns of Elizabethan England—that is, the issues and interests that shaped the playwright's own historical, social, and political world—permeate Shakespeare's portrayal of ancient Rome and the events the play narrates. *Julius Caesar* serves as a vehicle not just for telling the story of first-century Rome but for expressing concern about royal succession and its political implications in Shakespeare's England. Moreover, the play is written in Shakespeare's own language and contains anachronistic details that reveal more about Shakespeare's era than that of Gaius Julius Caesar. For example, in the opening scene of act 2, Shakespeare includes, for dramatic effect, the sound of a clock striking three—something that never could have occurred in first-century Rome. Thus, two important principles about how to read the play quickly emerge. First, the play must be read with reference to the language of Elizabethan England, not Roman Latin nor contemporary English. Second, the play should not be read as an historically objective depiction of the events it recounts. The play's purpose is not that of a newspaper or history report. Its object is to tell a story about the ancient past in way that reflects and responds to the culture, concerns, and interests of the historical world in which it was written.

We find a similar situation in the composition of biblical literature. Consider, for example, aspects of the historical world of Genesis 12–25, the saga of Abram and Sarai (who are later called Abraham and Sarah) and the first half of the patriarchal narrative of Genesis 12–50. The historical context to which Genesis 12–25 refers is that of the Middle Bronze Age in ancient Mesopotamia and the Levant. As the stories these chapters tell circulated orally for centuries, their composition dates to a much later period, perhaps as early as the tenth century B.C.E. or as late as the sixth century B.C.E. Whereas knowledge of the historical world to which the saga of Abram and Sarai refers may help bring the story to life for today's reader, the historical world of the composition of Genesis is relevant for understanding how and why the stories of Abram and Sarai were written and edited in the form in which we read them today. In other words, the rhetoric of the story—that is, how it was put together—reflects Israelite or early Jewish concerns, interests, and beliefs that postdate those of the Middle Bronze Age. For example, Genesis 34:7 reads, "When they heard of it, the men were indignant and very angry, because he had committed an outrage in Israel. . . ." Here "Israel" clearly reflects the consciousness of a period much later than that of the story itself, for at this point in the story, "Israel" as a nation or people does not yet exist. As this example shows, biblical literature often blends two distinct contexts— the world to which a story refers and the world in which a story is written—together.

Thus, each aspect of the historical world of the Bible signals an important way of approaching the biblical text. To readers at different times and in different places, various questions regarding the historical world of the Bible will be of more or less interest and concern than others. Exegesis does not require analysis of every aspect of the historical world of a text. Rather, it asks the interpreter to be conscious of the particular historical dimensions of the text that he or she is inquiring after.

The Contemporary World

The contemporary world, that is, the world *in front of* the text, refers to the world of the reader. It is less about how readers apply the text to their lives and more about how readers bring their world to the text. Because a reader's world is shaped by his or her social and cultural location as well as by his or her life experience and interpersonal relations, the contemporary world of the text is constituted by the constellation of values, norms, biases, concerns, presuppositions, assumptions, and expectations that shape the lenses through which individuals and communities read the Bible. What readers bring to the Bible largely determines to what their attention will be drawn and how they will engage the text that they are interpreting. This is not to suggest that the contemporary world of the Bible mechanistically determines a reader's interpretation. It is to remind readers that, in ways of which we may not always be completely conscious, our own contexts and experiences will shape the ways in which we frame, construct, interact with, and respond to the biblical text. In other words, the word takes root and moves within the lives of real people and communities who live and engage the Bible in the context of particular histories and cultures.

In order to look more closely at the significance of the contemporary world of the Bible, consider the example of how my college students have approached the story of David and Bathsheba in 2 Samuel 11 over the years. When I first covered this famous story in an undergraduate course I regularly teach, nearly all my students argued that the story centers on an adulterous love affair between the king and Bathsheba. In their recounting, the story sounded much like the 1951 Hollywood movie *David and Bathsheba*, which starred Gregory Peck and Susan Hayward, though, to be sure, none of my students had seen or even heard of it. Students' responses to the story began to shift dramatically first in autumn 1998 and then even more in spring 1999, when an overwhelming number of students asserted that the story of David and Bathsheba illustrates not an illicit romance but a king's misuse of power and sexual abuse of a female subject. Certainly the text of 2 Samuel had not changed. What had changed significantly, in the wake of the national scandal surrounding then President Bill Clinton and intern Monica Lewinsky, were student perceptions of, and sensitivity to, the dynamics of political power, gender, and sexual misconduct. The change in my students indicates how the context in which readers engage the Bible plays an essential role in shaping how they read and what they see in it.

The contemporary world of the Bible is not a private habitation. Insofar as each of us is a social being whose identity and experience is rooted in the multiple relationships, communities, and contexts that have shaped our lives, no one can read and understand the Bible purely as an individual. To some extent we always read the Bible in community, that is, alongside others, whether or not they are physically present with us. For this reason, the past several decades of biblical scholarship have seen heightened interest in and attention given to the social and cultural location of biblical readers. Multiple anthologies, as well as single-authored monographs, have taken up the topic of biblical interpretation by diverse readers in a range of contexts and communities. As a result, a diversity of approaches to the Bible, including African American, Asian American, Latino/Latina, African, Asian, Latin American, feminist, and postcolonial readings of the text, has been demonstrated and critically examined. Not surprisingly, globalization and the rich plurality of contemporary faith communities in the West and the rest of the world have underscored the importance of attending to the multiple contexts and communities in which the Bible is interpreted. The community of faith serves as the context in which the Bible is read and the word of God discerned and proclaimed. To preach most effectively, one should bring one's congregation into awareness when reading and interpreting Bible.

Ethics and the Three Worlds of the Bible

Because the proclamation of God's word is foundational to the life of the community of faith and the formation of Christian ethics, we must also consider the ethical implications of how readers engage the three worlds of the Bible. Since the literary, historical, and contemporary worlds of the Bible correspond to three different foci, the question of balance and integrity is pertinent. What is the relationship between the three worlds of the Bible? What makes an interpretation sound? What makes it faithful? What makes it ethical? If we are to take seriously the notion that faithful biblical interpretation should lead to the proclamation of God's word, then these are essential questions.

In seeking to provide readers an entry point into biblical exegesis that engages current scholarly approaches to the task, this volume presupposes that sound, ethical, and faithful interpretation balances attention to the three worlds of the Bible. While a sermon will often foreground one dimension of the text, exegesis during sermon preparation should not do so to the complete exclusion of other facets. Interpretation that focuses solely on the historical world, contemporary world, or literary world of the text invariably neglects the others. As Hebrew Bible interpreter Gale Yee observes, "What is deemed important to study in a particular investigation automatically reveals what is not important to look at."[5] Readers need to read the text conscientiously and self-consciously, that is, aware of what is being brought to the center of focus and what is being left on the periphery, and why. With that said, readers for whom consideration of the contemporary world of the text is a new concept should be especially careful to give that aspect of reading the Bible its due. As Yee suggests, "At stake in foregrounding the reader is one's ethical responsibility in reading and its concomitant political repercussions. This is especially the case in reading such a foundational work as the Bible."[6] Thus, ethical, pragmatic questions such as the following should not be foreign to the biblical interpreter: "How does my reading of the Bible affect my relationships with my spouse, my children, with others in my religious community, my social community, my national community, my global community? Does my reading help in transforming a society or does it (sub)consciously affirm the status quo and collude with its sexism, racism, anti-Semitism, classism, and imperialism?"[7]

Yet even as she argues for giving such attention to the reader and the contemporary world, Yee insists that what is needed is balance in approach and intentionality. Interpretation of the Bible is always an encounter with a profoundly rich and multidimensional collection of sacred writings, one that people of faith uphold as revelatory. As Yee shows, it should be an encounter in which the author, the text, and the reader both interact with and constrain one another. For in this incarnational and reciprocal encounter between the three worlds of the text, one may hear and become readied to proclaim the word.

Biblical Interpretation for Preaching

The following chapters build on this opening discussion by inviting readers to engage in a close reading of a biblical text and to explore various ways of interacting with the passage. Along the way, you will be introduced to key terms, concepts, and sets of questions that represent current scholarly approaches to biblical interpretation. By the end of the volume, I hope you will feel equipped to continue developing your own exegetical skills so that they can become a regular part of your sermon preparation and an enlivening practice of your own study of the Bible.

Chapter 1 guides you through a close reading of a New Testament passage to facilitate your attention to the literary world of the biblical text and to foster the articulation of the questions and expectations you bring to the Bible (the world *of* the text). From there, chapter 2 invites you to consider in increasing depth the contemporary world of the Bible and the context in which you and your congregation read and interpret Scripture (the world *in front of* the text). Chapter 3 focuses on the historical world of the Bible, specifically its ancient context (the world *behind* the text). Here readers will be introduced to historical and social-scientific approaches to biblical interpretation. Chapter 4 explores recent approaches that focus on the ethics, theology, and ideology of interpreting and appropriating biblical texts. The conclusion recommends ways in which readers may take a step back to see what kinds of data constructed during the exegetical process will be most helpful and relevant to the sermon.

Chapter 1

Bringing the Text into View

While the practice of reading actually engages all three worlds of the Bible at once, focusing primarily on one dimension of a biblical passage at a time makes the work of exegesis and interpretation much more clear. For sermon preparation, working in this way will make it easier for preachers to determine what aspect of the passage should ultimately serve as the thematic anchor of the sermon. Thus, with one eye on the pulpit, this chapter provides readers a guide for performing a close reading of the literary world *of* the text. We begin with the literary world of the text, which ought always to serve as the central orientation of exegesis, so that we do not unwittingly add to the text what is not there. Accountability to the literary world of the text is what most distinguishes exegesis from eisegesis.

The importance of the literary world is underscored by a key presupposition of biblical studies, namely, that biblical literature is the product of purposeful composition. None of the books of the Bible is a haphazard collection of thoughts and traditions. Rather, they are intentional and well-crafted writings. Bearing in mind that the overwhelming majority of the ancient world was nonliterate and that literature was read aloud to the masses, it is easy to recall both that those who knew how to write were among the elite and that writing was neither a common nor casual endeavor. The books of the Bible were written and edited by persons who brought intentionality and rhetorical skill to the tasks of composition and redaction. If for no other reason, readers ought to give close attention to the literary world of the Bible out of respect for the distinctiveness of each writing.

The overarching goal of examining the literary world of the text is to get the text in view and bring it into clearer focus. When an author composes a text, he or she constructs a literary world that includes textual markers and constraints that readers may recognize and with which they may interact. The author cannot control how readers actualize a text. How a passage is constructed in the reader's mind's eye depends upon the reader him- or herself. At first glance, this may seem so obvious that it should warrant little or no discussion. As is the case with many everyday activities, however, the commonplace often conceals a host of small but nonetheless important choices and decisions that we make. In both the everyday habits that we perform and the process of reading, such choices are replete with meaning that we assume and upon which we act. In other words, although reading is something that we do everyday, it is actually a very complex process. When we read the Bible, we are not just taking in words on a page. We are putting the words together, assigning meaning to them, and constructing with them a coherent form, such as a story, hymn, speech, or argument, in our mind's eye. As recent literary theory and biblical scholars have observed, reading is not a passive endeavor. By themselves, words on a page are simply marks on paper or pixels on a screen. It takes a reader to bring them to life. Thus, reading is a process of active engagement, one that we can describe as a reader's work in constructing a text, as well as his or her response to it.

This phenomenon, the construction of a text and its meaning, is well known to anyone who has visited a locale where one is unfamiliar with the dominant spoken language. The sounds of the unknown language, the gestures of its people, and the written word are simply that—undecipherable sounds, gestures, and marks on a page. In that rather lonely circumstance, a visitor recognizes that if he or she only knew the native language, then he or she would be able to "put together"—that is, construct in his or her mind's eye—what was being communicated. Reading the Bible is no different. In its original form, it is written in the languages of different and very ancient cultures that are unknown to the overwhelming majority of its readers. Most people read, or hear the Bible read, in translation. In chapter 3 we will turn to the question of the ancient context of biblical literature, but for now, let us examine how to bring the literary world of the translated text into clearer view. Even in English translation, the biblical text requires that we give our attention to how we read and what we make of a passage as we engage it. The discussion that follows focuses on an English translation of the Bible, namely, the New Revised Standard Version (NRSV), but the process that is recommended here is applicable to reading the Bible in its original language, translations other than English, and editions besides the NRSV.

Beginning a Close Reading of the Text

A close reading of a text begins with a narrow focus on the specific biblical passage, or pericope, that is under primary consideration.[1] Then the reader gradually widens his or her focus in order to understand better how the pericope relates to its larger literary context. The following steps describe how to get started:

1. Bring the Text into View

- Whether or not one is preparing to preach an already defined lectionary text, the first step in conducting a close reading of a biblical passage involves determining its genre or literary form. Is your passage either part of a story or a story itself? Is it an argument or illustration within a letter? Is it a hymn or an exposition? This is an important, if very basic, question to ask, for genre goes a long way towards shaping a reader's expectations.
- Identify the implied setting of the passage as well as the persons or characters that appear in it. Where does the passage take place? According to whose perspective, or point of view, is the text written? Make a list of the persons or characters or groups of characters whom you are able to name.
- Examine the contours of your passage—its beginning, middle, and ending. This will help you obtain a sense of the flow and logic of the passage. Try to determine why the passage has been delimited by its opening and closing verses. Often, the opening verse will signal a shift in time, setting, or action. Sometimes the closing verse resolves

the action preceding it, provides a short summary statement, or is followed by a verse that indicates a new shift
in setting, time, or action and the beginning of a new
pericope.

- Once the beginning and ending of the passage have been
established, determine the flow of the middle unit or units.
Outline the structure of the passage, from beginning to
end, in a way that makes sense to you. Soon you will begin
to see more clearly how the sequence of the passage
serves the argument or illustration it presents, the story it
narrates, or the poetry or hymn it contains.

- Identify what you see as the key topic(s), theme(s), and/or
conflict(s) that emerge in the passage. Pay special attention to the repetition of terms or the development of a
topic within the pericope. If, at this point, you find your
understanding of the passage's structure shifting a bit,
that is fine. Indeed, you may find yourself revising your
conceptualization of the passage more than once as you
make your way through this close reading.

Shifting to a Wide-Angle Lens
Once you have established a clearer sense of the passage, you can
widen your viewing lens and begin considering the pericope in its
larger literary context.

2. Reading the Text in its Literary Context
First, focus only on your passage's immediate context within the biblical book in which it appears.

- How is your passage related to the verses that precede
and follow it? Is it part of a larger argument, poem, or narrative sequence? If so, does it occur as part of the beginning, middle, or ending of that immediate sequence?

- How are the themes and conflicts in your passage (see
above) introduced, developed, and/or resolved in that
broader literary context?

After you have examined your passage in its immediate context, you may widen your reading lens even more to consider its relationship to the entire biblical book in which your passage appears.

- In what part of the biblical book (beginning, middle, or ending) does your passage appear?
- How are the themes and conflicts in your passage (see above) introduced, developed, and/or resolved in the biblical book you are reading? Note that your responses here may be similar to those you have previously named, but you should be focusing on different textual material in the overall book as you make the connections between your primary passage and the book as a whole.
- Are the characters that appear in your passage introduced earlier in the book? If so, how do you assess each of the characters in the material leading up to, and then at the conclusion of, your passage?

3. Optional: Placing the New Testament Text in Conversation with the Old Testament, as the Text Requires

Finally, in the case of New Testament exegesis, you may note what scholars call an "intertextual" relationship between your New Testament pericope and the Jewish Bible, or the Christian Old Testament. However, this will not always be the case. Intertextual material refers to content in the New Testament that is drawn from the Jewish Scriptures. It can pertain to quotations that are explicitly cited by a New Testament writer or to images, practices, teachings, and characters in the Jewish Bible to which a New Testament text either directly refers or indirectly alludes. Strictly speaking, observations about intertextual material underscore the intersection between the historical world of a New Testament text (which acknowledges the overall relationship between the New Testament and the Jewish Bible) and its literary world (which focuses on information gleaned from the text). When performing a close reading of a New Testament passage, it is helpful to examine any intertextual dimension of the text at this stage of exegesis.

- Does your passage quote, refer, or allude to material from the Jewish Scriptures? If so, identify the books, chapters, and verses of the passages to which the New Testament text is pointing.

- Examine each reference to the Jewish Bible, its original literary context. Identify what each Old Testament passage addresses or conveys.
- Now return to the New Testament passage and examine how it incorporates, changes, and/or makes use of the Old Testament tradition to which it refers. Consider how the older material gives shape to the New Testament text.

After reading the text closely in its immediate and broader literary contexts, step back and take one more comprehensive look at the passage. You may find the text even richer than before and, with each new reading, coming to life in a way that makes the text fresh and more accessible to you as you look ahead to the pulpit, the goal of your exegetical work.

Case Study: Luke 7:36-50

What follows is a close reading of a Gospel text, Luke 7:36-50, the scene in which a woman anoints Jesus' feet, followed by a wide-angle reading. As we examine throughout this book the various dimensions of biblical literature, we will return again to this Lukan passage. In so doing, we will see how even a brief exploration of the three worlds of a Scripture text can open it up in new and exciting ways for the preacher. Please note that this engagement of Luke 7:36-50 does not provide a definitive reading of the text, nor does it exhaust the approach outlined above. For instance, this particular Lukan passage does not include an explicit Old Testament intertextual dimension. The reading that follows here is offered in the hope that it will serve as an exegetical illustration which will encourage you to take up biblical exegesis with greater confidence and clarity about its purpose and usefulness.

A Close Reading of Luke 7:36-50

[36]One of the Pharisees asked Jesus to eat with him, and he went into the Pharisee's house and took his place at the table. [37]And a woman in the city, who was a sinner, having learned that he was eating in the Pharisee's house, brought an alabaster jar of ointment. [38]She stood behind him at his feet,

weeping, and began to bathe his feet with her tears and to dry them with her hair. Then she continued kissing his feet and anointing them with the ointment. [39]Now when the Pharisee who had invited him saw it, he said to himself, "If this man were a prophet, he would have known who and what kind of woman this is who is touching him—that she is a sinner." [40]Jesus spoke up and said to him, "Simon, I have something to say to you." "Teacher," he replied, "speak." [41]"A certain creditor had two debtors; one owed five hundred denarii, and the other fifty. [42]When they could not pay, he canceled the debts for both of them. Now which of them will love him more?" [43]Simon answered, "I suppose the one for whom he canceled the greater debt." And Jesus said to him, "You have judged rightly." [44]Then turning toward the woman, he said to Simon, "Do you see this woman? I entered your house; you gave me no water for my feet, but she has bathed my feet with her tears and dried them with her hair. [45]You gave me no kiss, but from the time I came in she has not stopped kissing my feet. [46]You did not anoint my head with oil, but she has anointed my feet with ointment. [47]Therefore, I tell you, her sins, which were many, have been forgiven; hence she has shown great love. But the one to whom little is forgiven, loves little." [48]Then he said to her, "Your sins are forgiven." [49]But those who were at the table with him began to say among themselves, "Who is this who even forgives sins?" [50]And he said to the woman, "Your faith has saved you; go in peace."

1. Bringing Luke 7:36-50 into View

We begin by considering the question of genre. The story that Luke tells here is not only part of a larger narrative, namely, Luke's Gospel, it also contains within itself a smaller story, or parable, that Jesus recounts in vv. 41-42. The setting of the passage, the home of a Pharisee (later identified in v. 40 as Simon), is explicitly stated in v. 36, "One of the Pharisees asked Jesus to eat with him, and he went into the Pharisee's house and took his place at the table." The characters in the passage are: Jesus, Simon, and an unnamed woman (introduced in v. 37). The point of view from which the passage is recounted is that of the Gospel's narrator. The brief parable in vv. 41-42 is told from the point of view of Jesus, the protagonist of the Luke's entire story.

The passage unfolds in a very interesting way. The opening verse (v. 36) signals an abrupt change of subject and setting. Following Jesus' closing statement in v. 50, another abrupt change of subject in the summary statement of 8:1 opens a new passage. Thus, the boundaries of its opening and closing verses clearly demarcate Luke 7:36-50 as a discrete pericope.

As the passage unfolds, readers may notice repeated shifts in foci. When one outlines the structure of Luke 7:36-50 accordingly, the following emerges:

I. Beginning (7:36-38)

- 7:36—Introduction to Jesus dining with the Pharisee and others.
- 7:37-38—Focus on the woman and her actions toward Jesus.

II. Middle (7:39-47)

- 7:39—Transitional statement ("Now when . . .") shifting focus from the woman and her actions toward Jesus to Simon and his thoughts about Jesus.
- 7:40-43—Focus on dialogue between Jesus and Simon. Contains Jesus' parable in vv. 41-42.
- 7:44-47—Focus on Jesus' gesture toward the woman and his words to Simon that compare the woman's actions toward Jesus to those of Simon.

III. Ending (7:48-50)

- 7:48—Focus on Jesus' initial words to the woman.
- 7:49—Focus on the response of others at the table with Jesus.
- 7:50—Focus on Jesus' final words to the woman.

When the passage is viewed as it is above, readers can see that the pericope includes two instances, not just one, of a story-within-a-story. As has been mentioned, the first instance occurs when Jesus briefly recounts the parable of a creditor and two debtors in vv. 41-42. The second example consists of the way in which Jesus' dialogue with Simon is framed by Jesus' encounter with the unnamed woman. Whereas Jesus' parable brings into sharper relief his dialogue with

Simon, so does Jesus' conversation with Simon interpret the interaction between him and the woman.

2. Topics, Themes, or Conflicts

Having noted the relationship between different parts of the passage, we may now turn to the key topics, themes, or conflicts that catch our attention. As repetition of phrases and topics sustains readers' and listeners' attention, the following can be observed as particular emphases of the passage:

I. Beginning (7:36-38)

³⁶One of the Pharisees *asked Jesus to eat with him*, and he went into the Pharisee's house and *took his place at the table.* ³⁷And a **woman in the city, who was a sinner,** having learned that he was *eating* in the Pharisee's house, brought an alabaster jar of ointment. ³⁸She **stood behind him at his feet, weeping,** and began to **bathe his feet with her tears** and to **dry them with her hair.** Then she **continued kissing his feet** and **anointing them with the ointment.**

- Jesus is in the home of a Pharisee (vv. 36, 37; underlined).
- Jesus is engaging in table fellowship with the Pharisee (vv. 36, 37; in italics).
- The woman is unnamed, but repeatedly identified as a woman "in the city" and as one "who was a sinner" (v. 37; in bold).
- The passage is interested in the woman's position, her actions toward Jesus, and her physical contact with him (v. 38; in bold and underlined).

II. Middle (7:39-47)

³⁹Now when the Pharisee who had invited him saw it, he said to himself, "IF THIS MAN WERE A PROPHET, he would have known **who and what kind of woman this is who is touching him—that she is a sinner.**" ⁴⁰Jesus spoke up and said to him, "Simon, I have something to say to you." "TEACHER," he replied, "speak." ⁴¹"A certain creditor had two debtors; one

owed five hundred denarii, and the other fifty. [42]When they could not pay, he canceled the debts for both of them. Now which of them will love him more?" [43]Simon answered, "I suppose the one for whom he canceled the greater debt." And Jesus said to him, "You have judged rightly." [44]**Then turning toward the woman**, he said to Simon, "**Do you see this woman?** I entered your house; *you gave me no water for my feet*, but **she has bathed my feet with her tears and dried them with her hair**. [45]*You gave me no kiss*, but from the time I came in **she has not stopped kissing my feet**. [46]*You did not anoint my head with oil*, but **she has anointed my feet with ointment**. [47]Therefore, I tell you, **her sins, which were many, have been forgiven; hence she has shown great love**. But *the one to whom little is forgiven, loves little*."

- Following the reminder that the Pharisee invited Jesus into his home (v. 39), there is sustained focus on the dialogue between Jesus and Simon (vv. 40, 43, 44, 47; underlined).
- References to Jesus' identity and character (vv. 39, 40, 49; in caps).
- Emphasis on the unnamed woman's character as one with many sins (vv. 39, 44, 47; in bold).
- Focus on the actions toward Jesus that Simon does not perform (vv. 44, 45, 46, 47; in italics and underlined).
- Repeated emphasis on the woman's position, her actions toward Jesus and her physical contact with him (vv. 39, 44, 45, 46, 47; in bold and underlined).

III. Ending (7:48-50)

[48]Then he said to her, "**Your sins are forgiven**." [49]But *those who were at the table with him* began to say among themselves, "WHO IS THIS who even forgives sins?" [50]And he said to the woman, "**Your faith has saved you; go in peace**."

- The focus shifts to what Jesus says to the woman, not Simon (vv. 48, 50; underlined).

- Focus on the unnamed woman's character as one whose sins are forgiven and whose faith has saved her (vv. 48, 50; in bold).
- A final reminder that Jesus is practicing table fellowship with Simon and others (v. 49; in italics).
- A final reference to Jesus' identity (v. 49; in caps).

3. Summary of Observations

Even a brief rereading of Luke 7:36-50 goes a long way toward bringing this passage into clearer view. At least four observations can be made at this point. First, the table fellowship that figures so prominently determines both the scene's setting and the context for evaluating the interaction between the Lukan characters. Thus, a theme that emerges in this particular setting is that of "place." Jesus takes "his place at the table" (lit. "reclined") in the opening verse (v. 36) and there is repeated interest in the woman's place, both literally (she stands behind Jesus in v. 38) and figuratively (in v. 39, Simon presumes to know just "what kind of woman this is").

Second, the passage also focuses repeatedly on the evaluation of the unnamed woman's character and reputation. The narrative creates a sharp distinction between Simon the Pharisee and the woman. Yet, even independent of such contrast, the text draws the reader's eye to its description of the woman. She is identified not only as "a woman" but as a woman "of the city" and "a sinner" (v. 37). Furthermore, as the narrative juxtaposes interest in Simon's thoughts and dialogue with Jesus with its steady focus on the woman's physical interaction with Jesus, the reader continues to "see" the woman. Jesus' question to Simon in v. 44, "Do you see this woman?" may be heard as somewhat redundant by the reader.

Third, the concentrated description of the woman's actions in v. 38 emphasizes the physical, even sensual, nature of her interaction with Jesus. Insofar as it follows the introduction of the woman as a "sinner," a reader assimilating the narrator's descriptors may tend to associate the woman's reputation with her behavior toward Jesus. Furthermore, the narration of Simon's thoughts in v. 39, "If this man were a prophet, he would have known who and what kind of woman this is who is touching him—that she is a sinner," certainly encourages the reader to view the woman with disdain and her actions as offensive. Simon's assessment of the woman also determines his view of Jesus, one that obviously turns negative. In Simon's eyes, Jesus has proven himself not to be a prophet.

The passage features sharp commentary in vv. 44-46 that not only reframes the woman's actions as expressions of hospitality rather than offense, it contrasts them precisely to what is lacking in Simon's response to Jesus. Jesus' words reveal the abundant love that the woman demonstrates (v. 47) and implicate the emptiness of Simon's own thinking. As the scene draws to its conclusion, it repeats the motif of forgiveness (vv. 48-50) and love (v. 47) that first appears in the brief parable which Jesus tells in vv. 41-43. Thus, what begins as a story hinting at scandal ends as a tale that exemplifies love and gratitude.

Finally, with Jesus' final words to the woman, "Your faith has saved you; go in peace" (v. 50), the scene establishes the unnamed woman as an exemplar of faith. Since the concept of "faith" is introduced at this moment in the episode, readers may look to the information the scene provides to determine of what the woman's faith consists. With its emphatic reference to the woman's actions ("she has shown great love," v. 47) the account associates faith with both the acceptance of forgiveness and the response of love. Thus, what sets the woman apart from Simon is both her vision of Jesus as more than an honored guest and her response to him. She sees that Jesus is indeed not only a prophet (contra Simon's conclusion in v. 39 that Jesus is not), but also one who extends forgiveness. It is faith in such acceptance and forgiveness that generates the woman's response to Jesus and, even more to the point, brings her to wholeness (v. 50).

This discussion represents only some of the observations that a close reading of the pericope of Luke 7:36-50 can yield. Since what readers will note in their engagement of the passage will vary considerably, it is important to keep in mind that the aim of this exercise is not to arrive at a definitive understanding of the pericope. Rather, the purpose of reading the text closely is to sharpen the reader's sense of the passage in order to facilitate an interpretation that maintains an intimate relationship to the text.

A Wide-Angle Reading of Luke 7:36-50 in its Literary Context
When we place our reading of Luke 7:36-50 in a broader context, namely, that of the Gospel as a whole, we can see how the topics and

interests of the pericope relate to themes that permeate Luke's story of Jesus. The scene occurs in the Lukan narration of Jesus' Galilean ministry. Later Jesus will begin his journey south toward Jerusalem, but at this point in the story, Jesus is carrying out his ministry in the region that surrounds the Sea of Galilee. He is accompanied by a growing number of disciples, including the Twelve.

Although Luke 7:36-50 is a discrete passage, it can be read in relation to the narrative sequence in which it is immediately situated, Luke 7:18-50. In the midst of the exchange that occurs between Jesus and John's disciples in the opening part of this section, Luke 7:18-23, Jesus says: "Go and tell John what you have seen and heard: the blind receive their sight, the lame walk, the lepers are cleansed, the deaf hear, the dead are raised, the poor have good news brought to them. And blessed is anyone who takes no offense at me" (vv. 22-23). Afterward, when Jesus turns to the crowd that is with him, he says of John: "What did you go out into the wilderness to look at? A reed shaken by the wind? What then did you go out to see? Someone dressed in soft robes? Look, those who put on fine clothing and live in luxury are in royal palaces. What then did you go out to see? A prophet? Yes, I tell you, and more than a prophet." (vv. 24-26). To this, Jesus adds, "I tell you, among those born of women no one is greater than John; yet the least in the kingdom of God is greater than he" (v. 28).

In Luke 7:31-32, Jesus compares "the people of this generation" to "children sitting in the marketplace" whose expectations not only go unmet but who also grossly misinterpret what it is they see: "For John the Baptist has come eating no bread and drinking no wine, and you say, 'He has a demon'; the Son of Man has come eating and drinking, and you say, 'Look, a glutton and a drunkard, a friend of tax collectors and sinners!'" (vv. 33-34).

Thus, in Luke 7:18-35, Jesus speaks to themes that reverberate throughout his exchange with Simon. Jesus repeatedly refers to "seeing" from the first scene in this larger narrative sequence ("Go and tell John what you have seen and heard," 7:22) to the last ("Do you see this woman?" 7:47). What Luke's Jesus emphasizes throughout is the importance of *really seeing*, that is, of truly understanding what one witnesses. When Simon judges negatively both the unnamed woman and Jesus, readers may be reminded of Jesus' preceding statement that "Blessed is anyone who takes no offense" at him and his provision of healing and good news (7:22-23). When Simon's responses to the unnamed woman and Jesus are read in light of Luke 7:18-35, he illustrates the very one who misapprehends and takes offense at the interaction between them.

The themes and motifs that appear in Luke 7:18-50 also occur in the Gospel as a whole. Indeed, all of the canonical Gospels make metaphorical use of sense perception, especially hearing and seeing, to express faith and understanding. As New Testament scholar Barbara Reid has observed, "Luke uses 'seeing' as a metaphor for perceiving the word of God" throughout the Gospel (see, for example, Luke 2:20, 30-31; 4:18).[2] The contrast between how the woman and Simon see Jesus, and how Jesus and Simon see the woman, develops Luke's emphasis on the need to "see" and understand. It also underscores the Gospel's concern for the "blindness" and ignorance that Jesus encounters throughout his ministry, and finally, in his death. However, in a Gospel that also emphasizes divine forgiveness, especially for what is done out of ignorance (Luke 23:34), readers may need to be careful not to assume that Luke 7:36-50 pronounces upon Simon absolute condemnation. For the Gospel does not narrate Simon's response to Jesus' teaching. It only lays before the reader the contrast between the woman's and Simon's initial responses to Jesus. It is the illustration of such contrast in which the narrative appears most interested.

Of course, Luke's preceding chapters also lend shape to how readers assess and "see" the characters that appear in Luke 7:36-50. By Luke 7:36, Luke has portrayed his protagonist, Jesus, as Son of God (Luke 1:35) who, filled with the Holy Spirit (Luke 3:22; 4:1, 14, 18), embodies and proclaims the good news (Luke 4:18) of the kingdom of God. Although Simon has not appeared previously in Luke, the Pharisees and other religious leaders have. Thus, when Simon is introduced as "one of the Pharisees" (Luke 7:36), he is cast among a group that figures prominently in Luke's Gospel. Although Luke's portrayal of the Pharisees is far from static, recurring motifs of the proximity, controversy, and contention between Jesus and the religious leaders permeate the narrative nonetheless. By Luke 7, readers are prepared to anticipate tension in the relationship between Simon and Jesus.

Taking stock of Luke's portrayal of Jesus and the Pharisees casts into greater relief the characterization of the unnamed woman in Luke 7:36-50. When she first appears in the story, she is portrayed as a sinful city woman. But as it unfolds, Luke's narration recasts her as a model of love, faith, and redemption. Together the woman and Simon form a pair that illustrates what Jesus' mother, Mary, sang about in her hymn to God. Indeed, Mary's Magnificat (Luke 1:46b-52) could easily be recast as the song of the unnamed woman of Luke 7:36-50:

> "My soul magnifies the Lord,
>   and my spirit rejoices in God my Savior,
> for he has looked with favor on the lowliness of his servant.
>   Surely, from now on all generations will call me blessed;
> for the Mighty One has done great things for me,
>   and holy is his name.
> His mercy is for those who fear him
>   from generation to generation.
> He has shown strength with his arm;
>   he has scattered the proud in the thoughts of their hearts.
> He has brought down the powerful from their thrones,
>   and lifted up the lowly . . ."

At this juncture, we should consider whether Luke 7:36-50 has an important intertextual relationship with the Old Testament. Does it quote, cite, or allude to any biblical passage in particular? And if so, how does Luke 7:36-50 make use of the Old Testament material to which it refers? Does it simply incorporate the older material, or does it reframe or change the meaning of the biblical image or idea on which it draws? If we find that our pericope does make specific and significant use of the Old Testament, then we will want to examine what this intertextual dimension of Luke 7:36-50 suggests.

When we place our passage next to the Old Testament, we can consider, for instance, whether the gesture of foot washing or the offense that Simon takes at Jesus' reception of the woman's touch bears meaning owing specifically to a particular biblical text or tradition. Does the image of the woman washing Jesus' feet recall the language of foot washing in Genesis (i.e., Gen. 18:4, 19:2, 24:32)? Does Simon's response to Jesus echo Levitical teaching about unintentionally coming into contact with human uncleanness (Lev. 5:3)? Whereas Genesis confirms the hospitality that the provision of water to wash one's feet expresses, it does not add significant nuance to our reading of Luke 7:36-50. Leviticus, which promises that the one who unknowingly comes into contact with uncleanness can attain atonement, addresses a concern that stands quite apart from Simon's. For the host's silent protest is rooted not in concern for Jesus, but in the ignorance that Simon presumes on the part of Jesus. It is Jesus' seeming lack of perception that scandalizes Simon. Many times, intertextual examination of a New Testament passage is fruitful. However, this is not always the case. With intertextual exploration of Luke 7:36-50 adding little to the interpretation of the passage for sermon preparation, the preacher should move on to the next stage of exegesis.

Conclusion

The literary world of the Bible is a product of the author's composition and the reader's actualization of it. The meanings that readers find in the biblical writings may indeed correspond to whatever their authors intended, but they may also extend far beyond what the ancient writers could have ever imagined. As canonical literature, the biblical text is highly delimited, but its interpretation remains quite fluid. In preparation for preaching, attention to the literary world of the text is not a means for arriving at a definitive interpretation of a biblical text. It is, rather, a means of forging an intimate relationship between the sermon and the Bible. The more you, the reader, lives with the text, the more grounded your sermon will be in it, and the more alive the biblical text will become for your congregation.

Chapter 2

Who's Reading and Whose Reading?

When we conduct a close reading of a biblical passage, we can begin to discern more easily the narrative and rhetorical patterns and motifs that have an impact on our understanding of, and our relationship to, the text. Having seen how a reader can explore the text in this way, it is to the reader's relationship to the text that we now turn our attention. Specifically, this chapter examines what biblical scholars call, alternatively, the world *in front of* the text, the reader's social location, or the contemporary world of the Bible. Variations in nomenclature notwithstanding, each of these concepts underscores that who we readers are and the contexts in which we readers engage the Bible shape our understanding and interpretation of Scripture.

Common experience attests to the significance of the reader in the interpretation of any piece of literature. For instance, whenever I ask a group of my students—who typically hail from various regions across the country and a range of backgrounds—to read and interpret a biblical passage, they offer significantly different understandings of the same text. Although they are enrolled in the same class, learn the same course material, and read the same study Bible, their interpretations will inevitably vary quite a lot. Or, as another example, who among us has not had the experience, when reading a text for the second or third time, of comprehending a familiar piece of writing in a whole new way? In fact, readers often find that their understanding of a text changes dramatically over the years.

Both of these everyday experiences underscore how the conditions and contexts in which we read shape the way in which we frame, perceive, understand, and respond to what we read, including the Bible. Congregations are filled with people who know what it is to come to a new understanding of a biblical passage after having read it numerous times. What changes over time is certainly not the canonical text itself. Rather, what evolves are the reading lenses through which individuals and communities view the Bible. At this point, one may well ask, From where do we get our "reading lenses"? What causes us to read and perceive the Bible in the ways that we do?

When scholars refer to the world of the reader, or the contemporary world of the Bible, they are acknowledging that the experiences, values, norms, beliefs, expectations, and concerns that together shape the worldview of the reader also have an impact on the ways in which the reader engages the Bible. Each of us brings to our reading of the Bible (or any text, for that matter) conscious and unconscious expectations of what we will find there and what we will take away; tendencies and associations that shape our understanding of the words we read; ways of constructing the text in our mind's eye; and a manner of responding to whatever we understand the text to be saying. The baggage that we bring is, in some sense, wholly personal. Yet it is also socially and culturally informed. Even in our private readings of the Bible, we read in the company of a "great cloud of witnesses," past and present.

The Reading Community

Most people tend to think of reading as a private, or individual, experience. They do so for good reason. We do the vast majority of our reading in silence, if not in private. As proponents of "the social location of the reader" remind us, however, each of us is a product not only of the experiences we have had but also of the various communities and sociocultural contexts in which we have lived them. The ways in which we are positioned socially, as well as the communities to which we belong and from whom we draw our identity, shape our worldviews, our symbolic universes, and our perceptions of "what is." Furthermore, the specific factors that constitute the social contours of our lives, including religion, race, ethnicity, gender, class, and culture, also inform our identities and perceptions. Because we readers are socially shaped and conditioned, so are our readings and interpretations of texts. Whether reading privately or for sermon preparation for a con-gregration, none of us reads in a vacuum.

It is not that one's identity or experience dictates one's interpre-tation of the text. Rather, it is that each of us reads with biases and none of us reads with pure objectivity. Thus, no single interpretation of a scriptural text can claim absolute authority, nor can it boast com-prehensive or exhaustive understanding of Scripture. Rather, every reading of the Bible, even one a community of faith deems especially inspired or insightful, remains somewhat contingent and contextual. Scriptural revelation is dynamic and incarnational and cannot be con-tained in or reduced to a single interpretation.

One approach to biblical interpretation that has emerged and grown in recent decades focuses particularly on the role that a reader's racial, ethnic, and/or cultural context can play in the course of interpreting the Bible. Culturally contextualized reading of the Bible, or cultural hermeneutics, explores the ways in which a reader's social and cultural context can and does give rise to particular questions and perspectives that emerge in, and have an impact on, biblical interpretation. A host of anthologies, articles, and monographs attest to the importance of this mode of interpretation in the field of biblical studies.[1] Whether focused on the context of world Christianity or the particular socio-cultural location of congregations in North America, these publications explore the factors that distinguish culturally contextualized readings of the Bible. Whether reading in the context of Nigeria, China, Latino and Latina North America, Asian North America, or African Amer-ica, for example, this kind of approach to interpretation illumines the encounter between real people and the Bible.

Interested in making the connection between the Bible and the communities of faith who turn to it for guidance and revelation, con-textual biblical interpretation often merges a theological (and biblical) commitment to justice and liberation with the analysis of factors that are frequently implicated in circumstances of injustice and oppression: race, ethnicity, gender, and/or class. The result is a complex discourse, one in which the construction of identity, race/ethnicity, gender, and class—either "in" the biblical text or in the lives of its readers—comes under focus. Gale Yee's observations about her own work in Asian American biblical hermeneutics highlight this dimension of interpreta-tion. As she understands it, her work emerges from an ongoing critical dialogue with dynamics she "had already experienced in real life: that there are insidiously complex interconnections among religion—based on the biblical text—and the 'isms': sexism, racism, classism, colonialism, heterosexism, fundamentalism, and so forth . . ."[2] Thus, rather than serving as a blueprint for, or a specific method of, biblical interpretation, Yee's approach represents a critical stance toward the task itself, one that exposes the relationship between religion, culture, and society. While Yee may focus on the meaning of a biblical text, she also takes up the question of how readers arrive at their interpretations, what they do with the interpretations they construct, and how their interpretations of the Bible have an impact on other people and communities. This particular hermeneutical approach builds upon the critical awareness that biblical interpretation both shapes and is shaped by those who read and engage Scripture.

Another approach that preachers may be especially keen to know is one that takes into special consideration the position and experience of ordinary, or nonprofessional, readers. These are persons and communities of faith who stand apart from the academy, seminary, and clergy. This approach not only examines and values the experience of ordinary readers, it seeks to integrate such experience into larger discussions of biblical interpretation and the question of whose perspectives are valued and whose are overlooked or even dismissed. Conducted largely from a liberationist perspective, it takes special interest in the interpretation of readers who find themselves among the marginalized and oppressed. For example, Bob Ekblad's *Reading the Bible with the Damned* examines "[t]he hidden transcript of the underclass in North America" and what transpires when "people become free to express this hidden transcript and bring it into conversation with the Scriptures and other fellow strugglers."[3] Here Ekblad writes in the company of those who have addressed the experiences and interpretative approaches of ordinary readers struggling in various settings across the sweep of world Christianity.[4] To read the Bible contextually is to take seriously that Scripture is composed, read, and interpreted in particular human situations and that the word comes to life anew in them.

The Congregational Community

The notion that we always read in community, or even multiple communities, is particularly pertinent in the context of studying Scripture for sermon preparation. For the preacher, the congregational community can serve not only as a primary context for interpreting the Bible, but also as a partner in the task. The preacher stands not only in the midst of more than two thousand years of Christian tradition(s), but in the company of a specific congregation, aiming to discern the word of God for the sake of, and in the midst of, that community. If the word is to be proclaimed as a living word, it will need to connect in a direct and intimate way with the congregation. Thus, the biblical interpreter who is preparing to preach will do well to bear in mind the "world" of the church community.

Distinctly positioned among readers and interpreters of the biblical text, preachers read both with and for their congregations. Reading *with* the congregation, the preacher engages the text with sensitivity and the aim of developing pastoral insight. Reading *for* the congregation, she or he searches the text for a prophetic word. Either approach to the text requires the preacher to know the congregation and its social, cultural, theological, and ideological contours and commitments. The more deeply you know your congregation and the more attuned you are to how they might hear and respond to the biblical text, the more mindful you will be able to be of those aspects of the text that might inspire, surprise, shock, or even offend your congregation. Conversely, you will also be more sensitive to those elements of the text that they might be prone to overlook or even ignore. To foster the congregation's experience of the Bible, you would do well to get to know your preaching community as well as your circumstances allow. As James R. Nieman demonstrates, knowing one's congregational context is key to shaping the sermon.[5] It is also essential to interpreting the Bible in preparation for the sermon.

Serious reflection on one's congregational community is no easy task and it is one that must be repeated on a regular basis. Learning one's community entails nuanced consideration of the social underpinnings of the congregation's identity, its recent experiences as a community, and its cultural assumptions. To examine these aspects of the congregation is to scrutinize values and ways of viewing the world that are ordinarily taken for granted. As Frederick C. Tiffany and Sharon H. Ringe observe, "It is not easy to begin to assess and define . . . cultural assumptions. These assumptions are so much a part of the environment that they are accepted as 'reality.'"[6] However awkward it may at first seem to take a step back from one's community to assess its social location, cultural identity/ies, and cultural assumptions, doing so will be of tremendous benefit to you. It will be especially helpful to you if you wish to discern: (1) the relationship between your community's social location and how they approach the Bible; and (2) the ways in which the social, cultural, theological, and ideological issues that the Bible raises do or do not relate to your congregation's situation and experience.

Whether or not a congregation explicitly identifies itself with particular social, cultural, racial, or ethnic contexts and experiences, it is, like all groups and organizations, shaped by such factors nonetheless. How might one go about the work of discerning a community's cultural assumptions and perhaps even begin leading them to do the same? Tiffany and Ringe note that "[o]ne way that people often begin to recognize the particularity and peculiarity of their own cultural assumptions is through an encounter with cultural realities that other communities take for granted."[7] The first approach could entail drawing on the same exercises that many organizations use to increase awareness of diversity and promote antiracist and inclusive ways of interacting. Another approach to this process of becoming more self-aware is to "try on" different interpretations of a biblical text and imagine how various members of your congregation and community would hear and respond to each interpretation. Both exercises may be an especially helpful exercise for majority congregations who may not be accustomed at all to thinking of their values and concerns, or their interpretations of the Bible, in terms of social context and cultural identity.

Biblical exegesis for sermon preparation involves discerning the living word that speaks in and through your encounter with the worlds of the text, its readers, and its author. Therefore, the congregational context, that is, the world of the congregation, is also *theologically* important. As Tiffany and Ringe suggest, "In and through this world God reveals God's self. This was true in biblical times; it is true today. Thus the world is a primary 'text' within which one can discern God's word."[8] In exegesis for sermon preparation, the preacher can listen for the word of God that emerges in his or her encounters with and between the "texts" of the congregation and the Bible.

Religious Experience, Biblical Authority, and the Congregation

A particularly important aspect of a community's life together is its collective understanding of its religious experience, including its relationship to the Bible and its authority. Religious experience and biblical authority are sources of authority that Christians often invoke but seldom articulate. Although what constitutes formative religious experience and biblical authority is difficult to define, how each relates to biblical exegesis for preaching is worthy of comment.

Recent publication on biblical authority attests to the multiple ways in which individual writers and traditions regard the Christian Scriptures.[9] For the individual preparing a sermon, what is of greatest importance is not whether the congregation views the Bible as authoritative, but what kind of power the biblical text holds for the community. An important dimension of exegesis for preaching, then, is consideration of *how* the Bible functions authoritatively in the life of the congregation.

To this end, Luke Timothy Johnson's reflections on biblical authority are helpful. He examines the subject with regard to what he identifies as Scripture's "three distinct functions," namely: (1) how "Scripture 'authors' a certain identity"; (2) how it "'authorizes' its own reinterpretation"; and (3) how it "provides 'authorities' for Christian discernment and decision."[10] In the first instance, Scripture is "read as a whole and regularly" so that it enters "not only the minds but also the hearts and even the bones, of its readers."[11] Here "the world that Scripture imagines" reshapes readers' identities and ways of perceiving. Thus, Johnson is keenly aware of the Bible's creative and transformative power in the lives of its readers.

The second kind of biblical authority that Johnson addresses "plays off the nuance of the Greek term *exousia*, which points towards 'freedom.'" As Johnson observes, the Bible allows and encourages readers to reinterpret Scripture. This is especially evident in the New Testament. Given the way in which it reinterprets Torah in light of Jesus traditions, the New Testament repeatedly illustrates the reinterpretation of biblical imagery and texts in light of religious experience. In short, the Bible itself authorizes the reinterpretation of Scripture for every age.

Scripture also provides wide-ranging "authorities" to which Christians may turn for discernment and decision making. Drawing on the analogy of the function of legal precedent in forensic discourse, Johnson underscores how multiple texts, traditions, and points of view constitute the Bible. They function as paradigms for the faith community to engage. Johnson argues that "responsible interpretation must take all these voices, all these perspectives and 'authorities' into account when trying to discern God's will in the present . . ."[12] Respecting and privileging the authority of Scripture is not a matter of mere proof texting. It is a process of faithful engagement.

Finally, and this is also key to sermon preparation, "authority does not necessarily translate to normativity." Whether or not a particular Scripture text should operate as the basis for normative faith and practice depends upon the task of discernment, a responsibility that goes to the heart of the Christian freedom that the apostle Paul proposed. For Johnson, this is precisely "where the 'authoring' function of Scripture enters: All discernment and decisions must be measured ultimately by their conformity to 'the mind of Christ' that Scripture in its formative function instills in the Church."[13] To this end, there may be no real certainty in decision making. The challenge, as Johnson reminds us, is not so much to make the right decision, but to make "decisions righteously."[14]

It should be clear by now that holding to scriptural authority does not alone address the preacher's task. Exegesis that respects the authority of the Bible takes seriously the interaction between the biblical text and the experience and witness of the body of Christ. Interpreting the Bible faithfully and with theological integrity is neither simplistic nor easy. But it is an essential task of preaching.

Case Study: Luke 7:36-50

Having considered your congregation's context, you may find it useful to return briefly to your initial reading of your preaching text. By taking even a few moments to retrace your steps, you will be able to observe your initial perception of, as well as your responses to, the biblical passage. As you note the specific aspects of the text to which your attention and interest have been drawn, you may consider which elements of the three worlds of the biblical text are most important for you to engage further. Finally, as you contemplate the relationship between your congregation's context and your reading of the passage, you may become more conscious of the challenges and needs facing the congregation that the text brings to mind. The relationship between the contemporary world and the other "worlds" of the text may help you discern the themes and ideas that will form the core of your sermon.

Another look at chapter 1 allows us to reexamine our initial reading of Luke 7:36-50. Our previous discussion of the passage focused on four main observations: (1) the primacy of table fellowship as the setting of the scene and the emphasis upon one's place at table; (2) repeated emphasis on the unnamed woman's character and reputation; (3) repeated interest in the physical, even sensual, interaction between the woman and Jesus; and (4) the reframing and reinterpretation of the woman's actions by Jesus that, in turn, served to recast the woman as an exemplar of faith. When the scene was examined in the narrative sequence of Luke's Gospel, we saw how the motif of sense perception, particularly that of sight, that permeates Luke 7:36-50 reoccurs throughout the Gospel as a key metaphor for faith. The woman whom the reader first "sees" through the eyes of Simon, the one who misapprehends her and Jesus, "sees" Jesus accurately and is herself eventually "seen" by the reader as a role model.

To retrace one's steps is not to discount out of hand one's earlier observations about the text. Indeed, chapter 1 demonstrated that the text supports the patterns identified above. The preacher revisits the initial assessment of the passage in order to illumine his or her encounter with it and to begin to discern the relationship between the passage and the congregation. For example, as I return to the textual patterns I isolated in chapter 1, knowing the likelihood that there are others that I could have observed but did not, I find myself wondering about the relevance of the themes and patterns to which my eyes were drawn. As I do so, I find myself newly aware of a connection between my social context and my reading of Luke 7:36-50.

My family and I are members of a largely white, middle- and upper-middle-class, urban congregation in the American South who has been called in recent years to overcome multiple legal obstacles, as well as some internal and community resistance, to establish and implement an overflow shelter in our church building for homeless men and women. In light of what we have experienced over the past two years,

I am sensitized to the theological, cultural, social, and class assumptions that determine the "place" of strangers in urban society and at the table of Christian fellowship. I am also more keenly aware of how homeless persons are sometimes "seen," on the one hand, as dirty, reprobate, sinful, and dangerous, and by some, on the other hand, as brothers and sisters who, as a group, are no more sinful and dangerous than the rest of us. In other words, my congregational context makes it easier for me to perceive and relate to those aspects of Luke 7:36-50 that highlight how easily the stranger, as well as those who interact with him or her, can be misperceived and judged according to others' assumptions and biases. As I reflect further on how themes in Luke 7:36-50 resonate with challenges that my church family has faced, I find that I am reading the Lukan text "with" my congregation. The ministry of those in our congregation and community who have stood with our homeless brothers and sisters also makes it easier for me to comprehend how Jesus' speech reframes the portrayal of the unnamed woman in Luke 7:36-50. Having witnessed the efforts and listened to the testimony of those who worked to make the overflow shelter a reality and volunteered at it this past winter, I am more aware of the power of compassionate vision—of seeing others rightly, or, to borrow from Johnson, of seeing others righteously.

Thus, even a brief reconsideration of my initial reading of Luke 7:36-50 in light of my present context allows me to imagine an encounter between my faith community and Luke's Gospel. As the purpose of exegesis for preaching is to engage the biblical text for the sake of, and along with, the congregation, one can also identify questions about the passage that may be relevant to the community. For instance, a reader can query whether there are other ways in which the image of "the stranger," "the uninvited guest," or "the unnamed" is relevant to the life of the community. Are there additional aspects of congregational life and experience that sensitize the reader to specific issues in the text? Are there concerns, or perhaps points of tension, over a ministry of the church that brings to mind the kinds of questions implied by Simon in Luke 7:36-50? How does the passage in Luke depict positions of privilege and honor? Are they relevant to the congregation? With whom in the passage do you want or expect your congregation to identify? Do you see your community as conventional or prone to judgment, like Simon? Or are they open and welcoming, like Jesus? Or would they more likely identify with the woman—the stranger and the one being judged? Note that you may answer these questions differently as the weeks and months go by, depending on the circumstances in which your congregation finds itself. Further reflection on any of these questions could forge a deeper level of interaction between the worlds of the reader(s) and the biblical text.

Finally, your reflections, questions, and insights will lead you to consider further additional aspects of the three worlds of the biblical text. Having completed a close reading of the literary world of the text and having noted where you and your congregation stand as readers and hearers of the text, you should consult the commentaries, sermons, and articles that other readers, including clergy and scholars, have contributed to the interpretation of Luke 7:36-50. Doing so will yield more information for your reflection.

You may also choose, at this stage, to focus on specific words, concepts, or themes in the text that require additional study or clarification. For example, Jerome Neyrey's study of meals in Luke-Acts explores how persons at table often fall into a kind of ranking.[15] Such insight could lead you to reflect on the dynamic of social posturing in the context of ancient and contemporary table fellowship. You may also benefit from an examination of the history of interpretation of the sermon passage. How has the text been understood in the past and by communities that differ from your own? Some of what you will find will no doubt confirm what you understand of the text; some may challenge your observations. In either case, consulting the insights of other readers and communities will both broaden and deepen your engagement of the biblical text. The important thing is to supplement your exegetical work with that of others and to resist the temptation to do the inverse. Otherwise, you will run the risk of arriving at an understanding of the text that stands at too great a distance from the particularity of community. Since one goal of exegesis for sermon preparation is to discern the living word that emerges from the Scriptures, the biblical text needs to be interpreted in the context of the life of the community to whom you will be preaching.

The Living Word

Taking the world of the reader seriously is a way of attending theologically and methodologically to the Bible as a means of discovering the living word that Christians proclaim. The Bible continues to speak in every age and context because communities of faith engage the text out of their own lived experience and in their own situations. With each new reading, the Bible speaks with a fresh voice, one that maintains continuity with those of previous generations of witnesses to the Gospel but also offers a word that is distinctive and very much alive. In chapter 4 we will address more closely two specific examples of how this hermeneutic circle, that is, the relationship between a community's life experience and the biblical text, functions in biblical interpretation and contributes to sermon preparation.

Chapter 3

Engaging the Text in Historical Context

As you examine the literary world of the biblical text and the contexts in which you and other readers engage it, you will likely encounter along the way queries, as well as assumptions, about the Bible's historical world. Careful engagement of biblical literature frequently leads readers to ask a host of questions about, for example, the ancient meaning of specific terms, the organization and function of particular social institutions or groups, the historical context of events that the text narrates or to which it refers, and more. To the degree that contemporary Christian readers continue to value some understanding of "what the text meant" to its original audiences, the ancient context of each testament remains relevant. For the preacher and congregation who are interested in connecting with the experiences and perspectives of ancient Israel or the early church, historical questions loom especially large.

As is the case with all language and literature, context gives rise to meaning. Thus, readers inevitably—whether wittingly or not—place the Bible's language, concepts, imagery, themes, and motifs in some larger past or contemporary context. For example, a native English speaker in North America reading only a current English translation of Luke 7:36-50 might bring to her reading of the passage a particularly contemporary framework and a familiar system of values. Problems can arise, however, if she wishes to assume that her understanding of the passage matches "what Luke meant" or "what the New Testament church understood." Luke and his earliest audiences were products not of our age but of their own. Thus, a reader can attempt instead to construct an ancient framework for reading Luke 7:36-50, in which case he might choose to examine what the motif of table fellowship might have connoted in Luke's time.

What matters most in exegesis for preaching is that the perspective your sermon adopts remains consistent with your approach to the text. If you want your sermon to be able to address some approximation of what a biblical text or its earliest audiences "thought" or "meant," then you need to consider the text's ancient context. And if you do so, you should begin with the language of the text, for the literary world of the passage often prompts readers to want to learn more about the historical context and meaning of the literary images, motifs, names, and social settings of biblical literature. Therefore, we will discuss the ancient social and cultural significance of the observations we made in chapter 1 about the literary world of Luke 7:36-50. But before we move to that specific discussion, we need first to clarify further what we mean by the "historical world of the text."

The Challenge of Historical Distance

When readers understand the Bible as Scripture, they read the text not as a compilation of past words but as a *living* word. Biblical interpreters debate whether or not hearing the living word depends on reading it against a particular historical context. When the preacher interprets the Bible for the sake of sermon preparation, that is, in the context of a congregation, he or she stands at the nexus of various historical contexts and engages all three worlds of the Bible. In turn, the gathered community tends to relate to the Bible on multiple levels. It envisions the Bible as at once ancient and contemporary, unchanging and dynamic, historically distant and experientially very near, foreign and familiar. Thus, biblical interpretation for sermon preparation neither simply replicates a past reading of the text nor denies the Bible's ancient origins. Rather, it considers carefully and intentionally the relationship between Scripture, in all its complexity, and the congregation, who both reaffirms it each time it is appropriated for worship and is shaped by it. Along the way, the preacher discerns the connections, tensions, connotations, and meanings that emerge and are most significant to the congregation.

Nonetheless, every biblical book was written in a specific time by particular writers in particular contexts. The stories that the biblical narratives tell also refer to specific settings. In turn, biblical literature has been read and interpreted, over several millennia, by real people living in diverse communities, specific historical contexts, and under various social conditions. The historical world of the Bible calls attention not only to these dimensions of the biblical text, but to the vast historical distance between contemporary readers and the various contexts in which the Bible was written and has been read in the past. In light of the undeniably historical context of the Bible, preachers face an important, if sometimes uncomfortable, truth about biblical interpretation: the Bible is both an ancient and considerably foreign body of literature *and* a familiar collection of texts that is often read with disregard for its history. Whenever a sermon aims to suggest, even implicitly, that it is looking to construct some sense of the ancient meaning of the biblical text, then it behooves the preacher to consider the ancient context of the passage.

Therefore, before preparing a sermon and determining what historical aspects of the text, if any, are most pertinent to the sermon, you should spend some time exploring the historical world of the biblical preaching text. As previously noted, the historical world of the Bible pertains to four major areas of inquiry: the historical setting and events to which a specific text or tradition refers; the historical context in which it was composed; the history of the text's composition and redaction (editing); and the history of its transmission and reception, translation, interpretation, and appropriation.

For the preacher, a significant benefit of exploring these aspects of biblical literature is becoming increasingly aware of how the text can be comprehended from various historical vantage points. To be sure, you will not find everything you note about the historical world of the text relevant to your sermon, but you will likely find that delving into historical data, to the degree that you are able in the time that you have, becomes an important part of the exegetical process. Historical consideration frequently expands and enriches one's sense of the text. Also keep in mind that although you may be moved to consider closely one or more dimensions of the historical world of the Bible, you will likely be both unable to attend to every historical aspect of the text and uninterested in doing so. Neither should you strive to incorporate into the sermon comment on every historical facet of the biblical passage. Selectivity is key. You should focus only on those historical aspects of the Bible that are relevant to your message. In the preparation stage, however, you should give some general attention to the historical aspects of the text.

History and the Ethics of Biblical Interpretation

A particularly important benefit of reading the biblical text in its historical context has to do with the ethics of biblical interpretation. Acknowledging that the Bible can be read in multiple settings intrinsically negates a simplistic and absolutist interpretation of the text. Reading it in its ancient context and respecting the historical distance that separates us from the communities and situations that generated biblical literature reminds us that we can replicate neither what the biblical writers intended their texts to mean nor how their readers understood them. Examining the historical world of the Bible places responsibility for how the past is envisioned and valued, as well as how it is appropriated, at the feet of its readers. Readers choose not only what they want to focus on when they read the text, but also how they want to construct "the past," namely, who's included and who's left out, which events or circumstances are relevant and which ones are not, and so forth. As we saw in our investigation of the literary world of the text, the choices you make as a reader have a significant impact on "the text" you are interpreting and the meaning you discern along the way.

In order to demonstrate the potential ethical benefit of reading the Bible in its historical context, let us consider the problem of anti-Jewish interpretation of the Gospel of Matthew. The Gospel, which is known for its inclusion of some of the most virulent, potentially anti-Jewish language in the New Testament (for example, "the woes" against the scribes and Pharisees in Matthew 23; and 27:25, "His blood be on us and on our children!"), has been used to fuel and even justify Christian anti-Judaism. Historical examination invites readers to consider Matthew's harsh language in light of the history of ancient Judaism. Whereas some scholars hold that Matthew's community was largely Gentile but heavily invested in the traditions of Judaism, others contend that it was itself predominantly Jewish Christian. Whichever the case, Matthew's reverence for Torah and his portrayal of Jesus nonetheless place Jesus squarely in the context of ancient Judaism. Moreover, given that the Gospel was written in the aftermath of the Jewish War with Rome (which resulted in Roman victory and the destruction of the sacred Temple in Jerusalem), we also know that Judaism was very much a minority religion in what was yet a very vulnerable position. If Matthew and his community were indeed Jewish, then we could identify the seemingly anti-Jewish rhetoric of the Gospel as indicative of intra-Jewish tension, that is, a "family fight" between competing groups within a shared tradition undergoing significant stress and transition. If they were not, then Matthew's harsh language may express the tension that emerged between some Jewish groups and another minority religious group which was, in turn, very closely aligned with Judaism (so much so, that to an outsider, they would have been indistinguishable). Whichever the case, the historical setting of the Gospel helps us understand a little better the dynamics that could have given rise to Matthew's rhetoric in his own context. And it helps prevent us from appropriating in today's very different environment the harsh language that one minority group used against another in a period when both groups were politically vulnerable. In no way does the Gospel of Matthew justify the history of Christian anti-Judaism that we have seen unfold over the course of Western history especially. In sum, engaging a text's historical context can expose that there are in fact ethical implications to examining or neglecting the historical world of a biblical text.

Reading in a Stream of History

Whenever anyone reads and interprets the Bible within the context of the church, he or she does so by entering into a long historical stream of biblical transmission, reception, translation, interpretation, and appropriation. Exegetes who consult biblical commentaries, encyclopedias, and dictionaries will find accessible introductions to the history of reading and interpreting the writings of the Bible. Indeed, preachers should have in their personal library, or locate a nearby library that has or can order, several respected reference resources to which they can turn when performing exegesis for preaching. Knowing something about how the biblical preaching text has been interpreted, either recently or in the past, enables the exegete to join a centuries-old conversation about it. As is the case in any conversation, you may find what you learn either inspiring, challenging, downright offensive, uplifting, or disturbing. On the other hand, you may find that commentaries and other resources for biblical studies confirm and deepen the work you have done on the text. Collectively, these kinds of resources invite you to be at once open to the perspectives of others and also aware of your own observations and insights into the biblical text. Therefore, commentaries should not function merely as authenticators of, or substitutes for, your own exegetical work. Rather, they should serve as resources and conversation partners that will help you sharpen and refine your own engagement and interpretation of the Bible. Before turning to commentaries or reference materials, be sure to engage the text directly as we did in chapter 1.

Examining the Historical and Social Contexts of the Bible

The mode of interpretation that has dominated much of modern interpretation of the Bible has, in fact, been that of historical inquiry. As interpreters became increasingly attuned over the last century to how biblical texts emerged in specific historical, social, and cultural settings and had histories all their own, they turned their attention to the task of examining the language and thought of the Bible in these contexts. It was simply not enough to study "what the text says." Rather, scholars began in earnest to seek the meaning and purpose of the biblical text in the context of where and when it was written, read, transmitted, and interpreted. They focused their attention on the relationship between the texts and communities that generated them, which, in turn, led interpreters to examine the distinctive interests of every biblical text.

Over the course of the twentieth century, such historical inquiry led to renewed appreciation of the distinctive theological character of individual biblical texts. A comparison of similar (or even parallel) texts, as in the case of the New Testament Gospels, illumines both the similarities and differences between them. Although each Gospel presents the story of the same individual, namely, Jesus of Nazareth, each draws its own distinct portrait of him. Thus, preachers may very well choose to refer not to Jesus, but to *Mark's* Jesus and *John's* Jesus, specifically. Close reading of the biblical texts reminds us that every text has its own message, personality, and theological perspective. Readers can learn quite a lot about a biblical text by reading it in comparison to parallel texts and reading it independently of any others.

An important mode of biblical inquiry that grew out of historical criticism emerged in the latter part of the twentieth century. Utilizing what amounts to a cluster of approaches that included social-scientific study of the Bible and social description of the biblical world, scholars introduced to the field of biblical studies a new lens through which the Bible could be read. Whereas previous historical-critical methods of interpretation had focused on the literary and theological development of biblical literature and the various communities of faith from which it emerged, these newer forms of social-science criticism used social-scientific tools not to trace a trajectory of historical development within ancient Israel or early Christianity but to understand more fully the social and cultural dimensions of the biblical text.

Thus, rather than asking what historical events formed the context for the Gospel of Luke, scholarship interested in Luke's "social world" inquired into the "meanings implicit in Luke-Acts through attention to the values, social structures and conventions of Luke's society which determine and convey those meanings."[1] By reading a biblical text in a way that captured its social and cultural context, interpreters began to focus on ancient "perception, expectation, values, social institutions, . . . modes of social interaction," and cultural scripts in an effort to bring biblical texts alive as *ancient* literature.[2] In recent years, an approach that focuses primarily on the interpretation of the New Testament has affected examination of the socio-historical dimensions of the text. Generally identified as "empire studies," this mode of analysis examines "the theme of empire as an exegetical lens through which to reframe and reread selected New Testament texts."[3] In the context of engaging Luke's Gospel, interpreters have studied "features which include economic relations, basic social patterns such as patron-client relations, institutions, especially the kinship group, first-century personality, peasant society, rituals and ceremonies, conflict and pivotal values such as honor and shame" to understand better "how the social dimensions of Luke's texts and context shape the author's perspective, compositional strategy, and message."[4]

So, too, the Hebrew Bible has been studied in terms of its social context. As a collection of disparate literary compositions, the Hebrew Bible "presents some very pronounced conceptual models and notions—for example, the idea that ethnic groups (Israelites, Moabites, Edomites, etc.) are extended families descended from individual male ancestors . . ."[5] Drawing on insights from sociology, anthropology, social history, and archaeology, scholars have examined the Hebrew Bible and the social and cultural matrix in which it emerged in terms of its institutions, social structure, assumed values, and presuppositions. By paying close attention to multiple social structures, including but not limited to ancient economies, city organization, and kinship, interpreters have been able to envision more fully both the literary and historical worlds of the biblical text.

Exploring the Historical World of the Text

As you begin to examine the historical world of your pericope, follow these steps:

1. Read the introductory notes to at least two biblical commentaries on the biblical book in which your passage appears; note the dating of your book's composition.
2. Read the commentary discussions of your passage or some articles on your passage. Jot down any information that catches your attention. Pay particular attention to topics and concepts that caught your eye when you examined the literary world of the text.
3. List any additional words, phrases, or concepts that pertain to the historical, social, or cultural context of the passage and about which you have questions that cannot be answered simply by rereading the text.
4. Look these terms/topics up in a major biblical dictionary or consult books and articles that address them and note what you find most relevant to your emerging understanding of the passage.
5. Reread your passage in light of what you have learned of its historical world.

Case Study: Luke 7:36-50

As you conduct exegesis for sermon preparation, you may find that historical and social-science approaches to the Bible help you engage Scripture by providing you a more vivid and accessible imaginative world in which to read the text. Therefore, as we continue our exploration of Luke 7:36-50, let us consider the historical world of Luke's

Gospel. To begin with, Luke's Gospel is generally dated from the late first century to the early second century c.e. Although scholars do not know specifically where the Gospel was composed, the Gospel's language and literary style suggest to many an urban sensibility and familiarity with the larger Roman world. When one takes into account that the Acts of the Apostles appears to be Luke's second installment in a double volume we might properly call "Luke-Acts," the author's sophisticated literary technique and knowledge of the broader world becomes even more obvious. In short, the Gospel of Luke speaks to an era in which the Jesus movement had grown into a largely urban, multicultural phenomenon. Moreover, as Vernon Robbins suggests, Luke's perspective is "emphatically bicultural; grounded in Jewish culture but competent in Greco-Roman culture."[6] Thus, the Gospel reflects and assumes a rather cosmopolitan disposition.

From the author's own words, readers learn much about the Gospel's purpose. The Gospel's Prologue, its four opening verses, make clear not only that Luke was aware of other accounts of Jesus' life and ministry, but that he felt it yet necessary to compose his own story of Jesus. In other words, Luke clearly found the accounts with which he was familiar to be somewhat lacking. Second, Luke understands that his audience is familiar with the story of Jesus. They were not what we would call today "naïve" readers. The third, and perhaps most important, information we learn from the Prologue is that Luke expects his Gospel to be adequate to the task of strengthening his audience's faith, the seeming aim of his composition. What distinguishes Luke's narrative from others is not the content of his Gospel, but the way in which he tells it. Luke understands that precisely because he tells the story of Jesus in the sequence and way it is best told, it will lend to its readers and hearers greater assurance about the truth of the gospel and their inclusion among the people of God.[7]

The story of Jesus that Luke tells is firmly rooted in the social and cultural context of the Greco-Roman world. Written for a majority Gentile audience, the Gospel utilizes language and imagery that incorporates the symbols and traditions of the Bible (which, in Luke's day, does not include the New Testament texts) and the cultural scripts and assumptions of his social location. In other words, Luke's feet are firmly planted in both the world of Scripture and the larger Greco-Roman world. The question remains, What aspect of the historical world of the text should we examine? Keeping in mind that when doing exegesis for sermon preparation, one's time is likely to be quite limited, be aware that at this juncture one needs to choose on what to focus. Clearly, not every aspect of the historical world can be examined. The choice of what to examine should emerge from your engagement with the literary world of the text and your sense of what is most relevant to your congregation. For example, if your consideration of the literary world of Luke causes you to become interested in the motif of table fellowship, then you will want to learn something of the customs and practices of meals in Jesus' time.

Thus, if we wish to examine the historical world of Luke 7:36-50, specifically in regard to the themes and motifs that we identified in chapters 1 and 2 of this volume, we should reread the passage again, placing it this time in the context of Luke's social world. Because the literary world of Luke 7:36-50 and the interests we raised in the previous chapters largely concern the social markers that permeate the scene, the social dimension of the passage lends itself especially well to further exploration. Table fellowship, references to the woman's reputation, Simon's thoughts about Jesus' own standing, and Jesus' emphasis on hospitality can be examined in relationship to the social context and norms of Luke's age.

At this stage of exegesis, it will be helpful to consult commentaries and other resources. Recent commentaries on the Synoptic Gospels, John, Acts, and Paul relay a great dealt of information about the social context of the New Testament in an accessible and concise manner.[8] From these, readers can acquire an overall sense of the conventions that dictated the behaviors of a host and guests at formal meals. A special meal "was held in two stages. The first, during which initial courses were served, was a time for servants to wash the hands and feet of the guest and anoint them with perfumed oils to remove body odors. In the second stage the primary courses of the meal were offered."[9] Such observation helps fill in gaps in the reader's knowledge of Luke 7:36-50 to make sense of both the flow of the scene and Jesus' comments to Simon.

Hospitality was highly valued during the Roman period, including the first century C.E. As David Gowler suggests, in antiquity persons adhered to a particular cultural script in circumstances where hospitality was extended. Hospitality not only oversaw the transition in a person's status from stranger to guest, it dictated a set of expectations that framed table fellowship. Respect toward one's guests and the avoidance of disrespect functioned as key dimensions of the host's responsibility. Moreover, anyone who was a first-time guest was afforded precedence over regular guests. However, a host's treatment of any guest was dictated by his or her social status.[10] Consonant with Gowler's observation, seating was formally organized according to the social status of the guests. Finally, hospitality also signaled the stature of the host. Indeed, "the whole community gain[ed] honor when one in its community host[ed] a guest of high status."[11]

The high valuation of hospitality is directly related to the centrality of honor-shame in this period. As something that was "understood as the status one claims in the community together with the all-important recognition of that claim by others," honor was a public affair.[12] Therefore, it functioned as a very important "indicator of social standing, enabling persons to interact with their social superiors, equals, and inferiors in certain ways prescribed by society."[13]

The Gospel of Luke is "full of small hints about the importance of behavior at meals. Thus, it is noted whether one washes (11:38), who eats what, when, and where (6:4), what is done or fails to get done at the table (7:38, 40, 44, 49), who is invited (14:12-14), where people sit (14:7-11), with whom one eats (15:2), and in what order persons of different rank come to the table (17:7-8)."[14] Understanding the social context enables the reader to more fully appreciate why Luke narrates such details and what they convey in Luke's literary and social worlds. That Simon and Jesus refer and respond to who is at table and how they behave is not, in itself, remarkable. What is notable, rather, is what each character makes of what they observe and intuit.

An underlying premise of Luke 7:36-50 is the potential fluidity of honor-shame. Whereas honor denoted the positive social status that an individual enjoyed, to "be shamed" was to lose honor. Thus, interpreters have emphasized the sometimes agonistic contexts in which honor was maintained, challenged, and confirmed. The social principle of "having shame" was a positive indication that a person recognized his or her reputation and the degree of honor it afforded the individual. Women, especially, were expected to have shame. Having no shame (as in the admonition, "Have you no shame?!"), indicated that a person lacked both honor and sufficient concern for this highly valued cultural script.

Returning to Luke 7:36-50, we can now see more clearly what is at stake in the scene, at least in the context of Luke's social world. As Gowler notes, "The dialogue between Simon and Jesus is an honor/shame contest. Simon can be seen as initiating the debate: his inward speech is an indirect affront (7:39). Jesus, however, answers the silent challenge and makes the debate public (7:40-42)."[15] Simon attempts to retain honor (7:43) but loses the challenge that he initiated. In effect, Jesus' response turns Simon's challenge on its head and Simon becomes the object of shaming.

Similarly, although Simon's inner thoughts about the unnamed woman cast her as a woman without honor, Jesus' response characterizes her as one who has greater honor than Simon. Jesus criticizes Simon for not supplying water for him to wash; yet the woman "wiped his *feet* with the hair of her *head*—the shameful task is done with the honored part of her body—kissed his feet and anointed them. The stress upon her humiliation is shown by the seven-fold repetition of the word *feet* in these few verses."[16] Thus, Simon loses honor by violating the requirements of hospitality in two ways: first, by not offering Jesus opportunity to wash; and second, by his silent criticism and judgment of his special guest.

Therefore, consideration of the cultural scripts and social meaning that run throughout Luke 7:36-50 brings the scene to life, so to speak, when it is read in the context of Luke's social world. The text's emphasis on "place" that we observed in chapter 1 is filled out when we relate it to the cultural values of hospitality and honor-shame. Moreover, we can see that when Jesus observes how the woman "has shown great love" (v. 47) and has been saved by "faith" (v. 50), his words signal a subtle but significant shift in Luke's focus. The value of hospitality and honor yields to the ideal of showing love and demonstrating faith. It is not that acts of hospitality and honor no longer matter, it is that they matter even more when they are infused with love and fueled by faith.

Reading a biblical text in relation to its ancient context constitutes a particular valuation of the past as a landscape of divine revelation. It is particularly useful when one wishes to imagine how the text might have been heard and received in its original context. Congregations who especially emphasize following biblical tradition or "living biblically" will find historical approaches to the text particularly relevant and meaningful. Sermons that draw on this mode of interpretation often focus on establishing analogies between the Bible's ancient context and the congregation's own circumstances. How do the messages presented by the biblical text translate in today's world, particularly in the life of a particular congregation? How does the ancient text speak to us today? Attending to the historical world of the Bible will help you begin to address such questions.

Chapter 4

When Worlds Collide
Reading against the Grain of the Text

When exegesis is carried out with attention to the congregation and the text, the reader will likely experience a significant expansion of his or her understanding of both the text and the way it may be heard by its readers and hearers. The preceding chapters have shown how even limited exercises in exegesis can lead to a much deeper engagement with the historical, literary, and contemporary worlds of the biblical text. But what is the interpreter to make of the text's relevance and meaning for his or her congregation? What if the text's apparent message raises one or more red flags for your particular congregation? And what if the historical distance between the text's context and your congregation's circumstances seems insurmountable? What if it becomes an obstacle to relating to the Bible at all? In short, what if exegesis leads not to a convergence, but, rather, to a downright collision of the worlds of the Bible? What, then, is one to do in preparation for the sermon? One may need to revisit the contemporary world of the text in order to give extended attention to the ideological and theological implications of reading the biblical text.

An underlying premise of these questions is, of course, that Scripture has a revelatory word for our congregations and that the Bible continues to hold authority for our communities. If we think back to our earlier discussion of biblical authority, we will recall that biblical authority suggests much more than a simplistic adherence to the literal meaning of a biblical text. Rather, it involves the church's twin tasks of interpretation and discernment. If the former is grounded in the kinds of approaches this volume is covering, then the latter is firmly rooted in the life of the Spirit. Discernment of God's word speaking through the words of the text cannot be reduced to a formula or methodological approach. Rather, to discern righteously the living word is to measure the words of the text in terms of what Luke Timothy Johnson calls "conformity to the mind of Christ."[1] Precisely because "authority does not translate to normativity," we must consider how one may respond to a text that seems not to conform to the mind of Christ.[2]

This question leads us to the phenomenon of what scholars often refer to as reading with or against "the grain of the text." Such language likens the text's point of view to the natural grain of a piece of wood or fabric. When a reader follows the general perspective of the ancient biblical narrator, then his or her interpretation will feel as seamless and as smooth as when one slides one's hand along a piece of wood or fabric in the direction of the grain. However, just as one feels a very rough or bumpy texture when one slides one's hand against the natural grain, so will the reader who asks questions or considers perspectives that did not occur to the biblical writer discover a "different feel" to the text and its interpretation. In either case, the authoritative biblical text does not change. What changes is the reader's engagement with it and the word he or she may discern along the way.

The interpreter who considers carefully the literary world of a text develops an intimate acquaintance with the shape of that world and the point of view that molded it. Examination of the historical context of the passage then enables the interpreter to envision a specific historical framework for the text's perspective. The question the interpreter inevitably encounters, consciously or not, is whether the point of view that gave rise to the text is one that continues to speak in a revelatory way to his or her contemporary context and congregation. Thus, the interpretive decision to read with or against the grain of a text is not a minor matter. It has significant ethical and theological bearing on both how you interpret the text and how your congregation will hear it.

Contextual Criticism

Whatever particular mode we may call to mind, insofar as contextual biblical interpretation (see chapter 2) highlights the context and role of the reader in interpreting the text, it also calls attention to the reader's authority and necessary role in bringing a text to life in the "real world" of a congregation or community. *Contextual criticism* reminds us that it is real people who engage the Bible on a weekly, sometimes daily, basis and it is they who grapple with the text's underlying ideology.[3] Thus, you may sometimes find yourself at a crossroad between the text's point of view and your own response to it, in which case you will be quite aware of the tension. A case in point will make clear what can be at stake in such a circumstance. The book of Joshua, the opening text of the Deuteronomistic History that tells the epic tale of the rise and fall of Israel, is inscribed with a point of view that depicts and justifies a violent occupation of the land promised to Moses. When one takes into account the whole Deuteronomistic History, one can see not only that Joshua plays a vital role in establishing the people's accountability to the Mosaic Covenant but that the book helps construct the entire theological framework within which the editor tries to make sense of the tragic collapse of the nations of Israel and Judah, which occurred long after the period reflected in the narrative but before the final redaction of the book. If one places the literary world of the Joshua in the historical context of the exile of the Israelite and Judean peoples, one can draw on the historical world of the text to explain and qualify much of Joshua's story.

However, understanding the literary and historical worlds of the text does not guarantee that one will perceive in its reading the presence and activity of the divine. Where, readers may ask, is the word of God in the midst of such violence? In answer, Rabbi Michael Lerner, who argues that biblical tradition retains both the voice of God and the voice of cruelty, suggests that Joshua's recounting of the violent conquest of the land of Canaan owes itself to the deep bitterness and pain felt by those who, centuries later, found themselves in exile under the Babylonian Empire.[4] In other words, Lerner reads the literary world of the text in relation to the historical context in which it was composed. But for Lerner, such consideration only further begs the question of what contemporary readers are to make of Joshua's rhetoric and ancient point of view. His conclusion, starkly and emphatically put, is that Joshua's account is not the voice of God but, rather, the voice of pain speaking in the guise of divine sanction. From where, one might ask, does Lerner draw the authority to make such declaration?

From biblical tradition, specifically those biblical texts that counter the violence which Joshua sometimes promotes. Thus, Lerner practices the principle of *reading the parts of the Bible in terms of the whole of the tradition.* His case is not unusual. Many readers of the Bible, Jewish and Christian alike, approach biblical interpretation with an inner sense of biblical principles and values. As Johnson suggests, the "world that Scripture imagines" shapes their engagement of individual texts.

Feminist Criticism

Whereas Lerner's approach to the book of Joshua represents a rejection of the narrator's point of view and an embrace of a larger perspective rooted in the Bible as a whole, other interpreters exhibit what some scholars call the work of a *resisting reader.* Rather than rejecting the narrator's perspective out of hand, the interpreter in this case reads against the grain of a text to uncover alternative meanings and implications that counter those that seem, at first, to dominate the text. Such a reader "reads a biblical or other literary text while aware of the standard reading and interpretation such a text receives in the academy, and then challenges that reading."[5] Recalling the Parable of the Widow and the Judge (Luke 18:2-5), preacher Carter Shelley notes how Jesus' story is often read through the lens of gender stereotyping and taken as an illustration of "how a woman's nagging can finally wear down the worst of scoundrels."[6] In response, Shelley resists this common interpretation to focus on how the woman's voice is that of persistence—not nagging—in the face of powerlessness. She then uses the model of the woman to call her listeners to "*act* through nagging, persisting, speaking on behalf of those allowed no voice, on behalf of those whose voice is discredited . . ."[7] In each of their interpretations, Lerner and Shelley convey a valuation not only of the context in which readers read, but of readers' authority to engage the text faithfully, even to the point of wrestling with it with no less ferocity than Jacob showed in his own struggle at Penuel.

Among various ideological approaches to the Bible, *feminist criticism* easily stands out as one of the most important forces in biblical studies over the past forty years. Insofar as it attends to all three worlds of the text, feminist biblical criticism has led biblical scholars to appreciate all the more the degree to which the Bible was written and has been read and interpreted by specific persons who are themselves products of a particular time, place, and culture. Since the cultures that generated and have received the Bible as sacred scripture have been largely patriarchal, a frequently "androcentric" perspective has shaped the literary world of the text as well as the history of its reception, interpretation, and use. Just like ethnocentrism, androcentrism limits the scope of a writer's and a reader's vision. The only way to correct such limitation is to become conscious of it. Thus, feminist biblical interpretation and other ideological approaches to the Bible seek to make readers aware of the factors that limit both a text's vision and readers' interpretations of the text. These approaches also construct ways to expand the reader's understanding of the text for the sake of both the reader and, in our case here, the congregation. Feminist interpreters, in particular, focus on applying a "hermeneutic of suspicion" to how the Bible has been interpreted and to biblical texts themselves. Such a feminist hermeneutic sees "androcentric texts as selective articulations of men often expressing as well as maintaining patriarchal historical conditions."[8] Thus, the aim of feminist interpretation is as much about exposing the ideological contexts in which biblical texts were written and have been interpreted as it is about the construction of new readings.

As Janice Capel Anderson emphasizes, "Feminist critics point out that just as theology, historical circumstances, and literary conventions shape" biblical texts and their interpretation, "gender shapes them as well."[9] Feminist interpretation of the Bible thus exhibits feminist conviction, on the one hand, and, on the other, a commitment to "the significance of the Bible, whether as possessing positive authority, needing exposure as a tool of oppression, or both."[10] With these dual commitments, this approach to biblical interpretation has succeeded and proven more influential than any other in exposing the ideological grain of biblical texts and traditions and in helping readers of faith respond to it. In her excellent summary of feminist biblical scholarship, Capel Anderson identifies three modes of "feminist critique" and four modes of "feminist construction." The modes of feminist critique are:

1. critique of the androcentric and patriarchal character of the Bible;

2. critique of the androcentric and patriarchal character of biblical interpretation; and
3. countering passages that legitimate or have been used to legitimate oppression with counterpassages or liberating interpretations of such passages.[11]

Whereas the first two focus on exposing the limited vision of the biblical writers and their interpreters, the latter seeks to bring to readers' attention texts that themselves go against the grain of androcentrism and patriarchy. Thus, its goal is to expand readers' understanding of "what the text says." This approach also seeks to reinterpret familiar passages in ways that bring to light alternative textual or reading perspectives which shed new light on the text.

The modes of feminist construction that Capel Anderson cites are:

1. recovering female images of God and concentrating on stories of women in the text in order to recover images of biblical women, images of agency, and images of victimization;
2. rewriting the histories of Israel and the early church;
3. recovering the history of women interpreting the Bible and rewriting the history of interpretation; and
4. examining readers' responses.[12]

The first mode recognizes that there is also much in the Bible that counters male exclusive images of God and patriarchal portrayals of women. Recognizing the richness of biblical tradition, it seeks to retrieve the images of God and women in the Bible that readers and interpreters have too often overlooked. The second and third approaches aim to rewrite and retell the histories of Israel, early Christianity, and biblical interpretation in light of what feminist scholars have recovered of women's history and women's interpretation of the Bible over the centuries. Finally, the fourth mode examines the ways in which readers, past and present, have responded to the Bible: "A particularly important question for many religious feminists is how the Bible has empowered women readers and hearers in the past and how it might continue to do so, despite its patriarchy and androcentrism. Or, how

have women read or heard the Bible so it has been a source of affirma-
tion and power for them?"[13] Thus, feminist biblical interpretation takes
a critical stance toward the ideology that so often undergirds biblical
tradition at the same time that it acknowledges the Bible's power to
overcome such limitation in its impact on real persons' lives.

Postcolonial Interpretation

Postcolonial biblical interpretation is a more recent mode of criticism
that also addresses the ideologies of biblical texts and their interpretation. Unlike feminist approaches to the Bible, postcolonial interpretation
focuses less on specific methodologies and more on a general consciousness that one may bring to one's engagement of Scripture. This
kind of approach differs from older liberationist modes of interpretation insofar as it "sees the Bible as at once a source of emancipation
and a source of oppression." Thus, whereas some scholars stress the
antiimperial and anticolonial theology that one finds in biblical tradition,
others focus on how the Bible ultimately reinforces the very imperial
and colonial tendencies it sometimes seeks to counter.

Largely related to contextual readings of the Bible, postcolonial
interpretation stresses both fresh ways of reading the Bible and critique of the ways in which the Bible has been interpreted and used to
promote the ideologies and values of a largely individualistic Western
Christianity. Close attention is paid to the history of the Bible's reception and interpretation and the ways in which past readings of biblical
literature have obscured aspects of the text. Thus, Stephen D. Moore
cites the work of Musa Dube as an example of a strong postcolonial
sensibility:

> Writing explicitly out of a Botswanan, and, more generally, black Afri-
> can cultural context, Dube enacts a 'decolonizing' feminist reading of
> the exodus and conquest narratives in the Hebrew Bible, together with
> selected Matthean narratives, especially Jesus' enigmatic encounter with
> the 'Canaanite' woman; provides a devastating critique of previous read-
> ings of the latter pericope by white European-American interpreters, not
> least feminist interpreters; and champions non-academic readings of the
> pericope . . . [14]

Dube, for example, draws on the book of Joshua to demonstrate how Rahab serves as an example of a woman who betrays her own people and represents the "projected desire of the colonizer."[15] Rahab is a heroine only when her story is read without any attention to the imperialist ideology that runs through the biblical text.

Therefore, feminist, contextual, and postcolonial biblical interpretations of the Bible demonstrate how readers can resist reading with the grain of the biblical text. By reading against the grain of either the text or the history of its interpretation, each of these approaches seeks to expose the ideological underpinnings of biblical literature. They also promote ways of engaging the Bible that either acknowledges the tension between ancient texts and contemporary readers or offers alternative readings of the text. Many strive to acknowledge and understand how the Bible, despite its very human limitations, can be read in a manner that speaks to real people in powerful and life-affirming ways.

Reading with Resistance

To read the biblical text as a resisting and faithful reader is to consider a passage in the contexts of the three worlds of the Bible and assess it in terms of the biblical values of liberation and social justice. To readers for whom the biblical tradition is a witness to these values, reading with resistance is both a way of countering a history of sometimes oppressive readings of the Bible and a means of living out one's faith. It is often a vehicle for theological interpretation of the text. To become more aware of how your reading of the text could affect others, explore the following steps:

1. Jot down any new observations and responses. What does the text seem to be saying or doing?
2. Reflect on the implications of your reading.

   • First, consider how various persons and groups in your family and congregation could hear and respond to your reading of the text. What impact would it have on them? Would it affect them in ways that differ from its implications for you and your life?

- Now reflect on how various persons and groups in your local community, and then in the wider national and global community, could hear and respond to your reading of the text. What impact would it have on them? Would it affect them in ways that differ from its implications for you and your life? Whose interests does the ideological grain of the text serve or reflect, and whose does it overlook?

3. Do you find yourself reading with or against the grain of the text? How and why? Are you wanting to revisit your examination of any particular dimension of the text?
4. Continue exploring the relationship between the text and you and your congregation. What does your response and your congregation's likely response reveal about the text? What does it reveal about you and your congregation? What word are you hearing from the text?

Case Study: Luke 7:36-50

When one interprets the Bible for sermon preparation, time limitations generally prohibit extensive consideration of the approaches that this chapter has introduced. Here, again, the interpreter needs to choose what she or he will focus on for this particular sermon, knowing that a different approach to the same text can be taken in the future. A good way to choose from among various modes of interpretation is to return to the close reading of the text with which the interpreter began. The preacher should consider which approach will best suit the observations that have already been made. In the case of our present reading of Luke 7:36-50, a feminist approach to the passage will allow us to examine more closely the scene and its main characters, especially the unnamed woman.

Let us return now to Luke 7:36-50. Having engaged the three worlds, including the social dimension, of Luke 7:36-50, questions about the text's portrayal of the unnamed woman in the story and its overarching view remain to be addressed. The narrator clearly views the woman positively and, specifically, as a model of faith. We may ask, however, What constitutes that "positive" vision of the woman? In other words, what do we really know about her? If Luke has us seeing her through the eyes of other male characters, how might our impression of her be shaped by Simon's perspective? Should the reader simply adopt the perspective of the narrator? Can the reader even resist the limited framework in which his imagination places the woman?

It is to these kinds of questions that Barbara E. Reid turns as she "attempts to unmask the gender biases that have shaped both the text and our interpretations of it."[16] As she argues, "Such an approach challenges us to look with new eyes and to excise cataracts formed from misperceptions, prejudgments, and stereotyped views of women that blind us to the full identity of Jesus. Reading Luke in this way, however, is not in conformity with the evangelist's intent."[17] Thus, to read against the grain of a text is to work with and through it but in a way that the text itself does not encourage. For the preacher and the congregation, this means acknowledging the authority not only of Scripture but of the reader as well. Theologically, it points to the movement of the Spirit and the liveliness of interpreting a canon of living texts into which every generation of faith breathes new life.

Feminist engagement of Luke 7:36-50 underscores both the language of Luke's description of the unnamed woman and her interaction with Jesus and the interpretive assumptions and moves that readers make as they engage the scene. After reading through a host of interpretations of Luke 7:36-50, Teresa J. Hornsby finds herself wondering, "What is it about Luke's narrative that makes readers want to identify the woman as a prostitute?"[18] Her own initial interpretation of the scene picks up on the same physicality and emotion that we, too, identified in chapter 1. Similarly, such narrative detail leads Hornsby to conclude not that the woman is a prostitute, but that she is independent and unhindered by convention, someone able to "[blend] together the movements of her body with an expression of raw emotion."[19] Citing Jesus' response to the woman, Hornsby concludes that the Gospel confirms her construction of the scene.

However, Hornsby also sees that the history of interpretation conveys a divergent reading of the woman. She writes:

> With very few exceptions, especially in any work prior to the mid-1980s, scholars either call her a prostitute or they claim that the label the narrator gives her of 'sinner' . . . surely indicates that the anointing woman is a carnal

transgressor; her effusive weeping, they write, must be indicative of sexual, shame-inspired remorse and repentance; her ointment must have come from her prostitute's tool-box; and the fact that she is kissing a strange man can only mean that she is sexually immoral. Luke's male sinners, even those who weep or who are specifically linked to prostitutes, do not acquire the taint of shame comparable to that of the anointing woman.[20]

Hornsby examines the gaps in Luke's narrative (what are readers to make of the designation of the woman as a "sinner" and her presence at the meal that Simon hosts?) and how readers fill them. She concludes that readers bring their stereotypes and assumptions about women and sexual immorality to the text in a way that transforms its emphasis on the woman's physicality. Her story, in short, "has been retold in ways that displace her, render her behavior as excessive, [negatively] sexualize her, and present her as deviant. Her character is reconstructed in order to appropriate her body and thus neutralize the perceived threat of the woman's physicality."[21] Thus, Hornsby's analysis of Luke 7:36-50 underscores the sexism that permeates the history of the text's interpretation.

As feminist interpreters, Hornsby and Reid expose the choices that readers make as they interact with Luke 7:36-50. Where Hornsby focuses on the analysis of readers' responses to the text, Reid takes up the matter of fashioning a feminist approach to its interpretation. Because of its interest in identifying and speaking to the ideological grain of the text, feminist interpretation of Luke 7:36-50 begins with critical engagement with the literary and historical worlds of the text. Like Hornsby, Reid queries the lenses through which readers see the text, but she begins with the question, "Through whose lenses has the text been constructed and under what historical circumstances?"[22] She then recommends that after answering these initial questions, that readers take up the following: "What is wrong with this picture? How does the portrait of women presented by Luke match or contrast with contemporary women's experience?"[23] Here Reid underscores the premise of feminist biblical interpretation, the starting point that has given rise to contextual and postcolonial readings of the Bible, namely, that readers matter. And they draw authority from their lived experience.

Reid's line of questioning recommends examining where the text is leading the reader, what tools the reader needs in order to render the text meaningful in a new context, and whether the reader is willing to read the text in a new way. Her aim is to enable readers to be led to what she calls "open horizons." Though the space may be a new one for her readers, it is not without precedent in biblical tradition or the field of biblical studies. Drawing on Elisabeth Schüssler Fiorenza's work, Reid argues, "We find ourselves at a new juncture not unlike the position of Jesus' first women disciples. Having witnessed the death of the Jesus they had come to know and believe in, the women entered the open space of the empty tomb, which impelled them forward to unimaginable new horizons."[24] Just as the women at the empty tomb were told to find Jesus in Galilee where he had gone ahead of them, so may Luke's readers move forward to encounter Jesus on the interpretive journey that awaits.

Although a feminist reading of Luke 7:36-50 may lead to a new rendering of the passage, its primary aim, as Hornsby and Reid illustrate, is to interrogate Luke's narration of the scene and the way in which readers engage it. In so doing, of course, readers may also call on the social meaning and cultural scripts of the passage, or other data drawn from the historical world of the text. What changes most in feminist interpretation is the inclusion of the reader and the significance of woman's lived experience in the interpretation and appropriation of the text. This means that the message the exegete ultimately takes from the passage may focus on Luke's rendering of the text, a new reading of the scene, a revelatory word derived from a feminist examination of how the text has been, or continues to be, read, or a combination.

These possibilities underscore precisely what makes feminist interpretation such an important approach for preachers to consider. Feminist interpretation for preaching affirms the congregation, not just the Scripture nor Scripture in isolation, as the locus of divine revelation. It is the Bible *as it is read and as it takes root in the lives of a community of faith* with which this approach is most concerned. Thus, a feminist approach to Luke 7:36-50 could lead to a sermon on either Luke's story, the interpretation of Luke's story, or what we can learn theologically about ourselves as readers and our ways of seeing the biblical text.

Conclusion
Discerning the Transforming Word

Reading is not a straightforward, linear process, and exegesis is not a science. When readers engage the biblical text, they repeatedly cross boundaries between, and move in and out of, its three worlds. In the practice of reading, one cannot truly isolate the worlds of the text, behind the text, and in front of the text from one another. All three function simultaneously. Focusing on one dimension of the text at a time, as the previous chapters have done, is a reading strategy that provides the interpreter a way to concentrate his or her attention on one specific aspect of the Bible at a time. Thus, it enables readers to engage the text more deliberately and self-consciously. Doing so may especially help readers preparing to preach because it affords one the opportunity to become increasingly attuned not only to the text but to the relationship that forms between the reader, text, and congregation.

As the previous chapters have shown, whenever you interpret the Bible, you are likely to negotiate several options in reading. As your reading brings the text to life, so to speak, you will be making multiple choices along the way. You will have to determine, for example, what in the text is important to note, what can be overlooked, what certain words and phrases mean, whether they are relevant to the congregation, and if so, how. You may rarely, nor need you always, be fully aware of why you are drawn to certain details and aspects of a biblical passage. For although some choices are conscious, typically many are not. Moreover, you will often be unaware of those dimensions of the text to which you are not attending. The approach to biblical interpretation that this volume presents aims to help you become better able to observe such choices and reflect on them. Such exegesis sheds light not only on the text but on the reader and the context in which he or she engages the biblical text.

The exegetical exercises that this volume presents signal a particular way of conceiving of the task of exegesis. Together they affirm biblical exegesis as both a means of relating to and constructing the biblical text, and a process by which the preacher may be led to reflect as much on the congregation and its circumstances as on the biblical text. For somewhere in the midst of exegesis, most preachers will find themselves both rethinking their conception of the text and revisiting their understanding of the faith community. Just as exegesis takes the preacher "deeper" into the text, so can it lead him or her to careful consideration of the community with and for whom the text is being interpreted.

Toward Interpretation

Once one has studied all three worlds of the biblical text, the question arises, "What next?" What does one do with all the data that the initial exegetical process yields? And *how does one move from constructing and gathering all kinds of interesting information about the text, including its rhetorical patterns and motifs, literary setting, history, reception, and contemporary audience, toward a concise interpretation of the text that can, in turn, become the basis of the sermon?* The question is an important one, not least because it brings the reader back to the very reason for engaging the text to begin with, namely, the sermon and the congregation.

As an interpreter, you will need to decide between several points of orientation to the biblical text you are reading. Turning toward the task of interpretation entails choosing from among at least four related, but different, foci:

1. what the text says or means;
2. how the text says or means;
3. how the preacher (and congregation) reads and makes sense of the text; or
4. what the text reveals about the preacher and congregation.

If you decide to focus your interpretation on what the text says or means, you will select data from your engagement with the world(s) of the text that helps you read either with or against the logic and point of view of the text. For example, if you are going to preach on the story of Hagar and Ishmael in Genesis 21:8-21, your interpretation could focus on how the story unfolds as, for example, a story of God's compassion for the oppressed slave and her child. On the other hand, your interpretation could read against the grain of the text and focus on the patriarchal social values and gender roles that set up the situation to which Sarah responds. In this light, the interpretation could serve as a critique of the patriarchy that dominates the stories of the foremothers and forefathers of Israel following the story of the expulsion from the garden in Genesis 3.

Alternatively, you could decide instead to steady your interpretation not on what the story says but on how it is told or put together. Here you could concentrate on how the text begins but then abandons its initial focus on Sarah in order to highlight the experience and perspective of the slave woman, Hagar, and her son, and you could interpret the significance of such a rhetorical shift. In so doing, you would draw on the data you have culled from your initial exegetical consideration of the text to follow the rhetoric of the passage in the way that the text presents it. You might draw specific conclusions about the text's focus on Hagar. For example, you may conclude that the text's rhetorical shift mirrors the divine compassion of which it tells.

Instead of attending only to the text's presentation of the story, you could choose alternatively to focus on the choices that you and your congregation, as readers, navigate as you read Genesis. If there are obvious ambiguities and gaps in the story, you could identify these and discuss how readers can fill them. You could focus on whatever words and phrases in the pericope catch your attention and examine them carefully. You could then even choose to rewrite or paraphrase the story as a way of interpreting it.

Rather than staying with how you read Genesis 21, you could focus on how the way in which you and your congregation read and respond to the text reveals something about your community and your own situation and biases. Were you surprised by the text's shift in focus from Sarah to Hagar, or had you been wanting the narrator to turn your attention to Hagar? With whom did you most empathize or identify? Did you miss greater attention to Abraham? How do you envision the rest of Hagar's life to which the passage's concluding summary statement points? Consideration of these questions and others would give you much to ponder regarding the relationship between the text and your community. What can the biblical text teach you about yourselves and what is the relationship between your community's identity and social location and the text's message? Does the text affirm, challenge, disturb, or inspire your congregation?

Each of these angles will yield a different interpretation of the text, yet each is certainly a valid approach to exegesis. Remember that the interpretation you offer in the pulpit ought not be a report of all you have learned in the study. You must make choices. Your sermon will be only as effective as it is focused. If you find it especially difficult to decide what to focus on and what to let go of, bear in mind that you can preach on a text more than once. Save your notes for another sermon and begin turning your attention to the next task at hand, which is to move from interpreting the biblical text to discerning the central word you are being led to preach.

Discerning the Word

Moving from interpretation to a word that will serve as the center of your sermon requires narrowing your focus further. For you now need to discern the idea or theme that you want to take from your exegetical work to your sermon preparation. You should, at this stage, know which interpretive stance you are taking toward the text and whether you are focusing on what the text says or means, how the text says or means, how the preacher (and congregation) reads and makes sense of the text, or what the text reveals about the preacher and congregation. The aim of this stage of your work is to discern a key idea around which you can build your sermon. From this key idea you can shape a fully developed sermonic claim and rhetorical strategy for your sermon.[1]

Let us return to my first example in the previous discussion of how to focus one's interpretive work. If you were to attend primarily to what Genesis 21:8-21 says and if the focus of your interpretation has been on God's compassion, then the word you discern and take to the composition of your sermon will be related to that general theme. You could, for example, land on v. 17 as the key idea of your sermon: "And God heard the voice of the boy; and the angel of God called to Hagar from heaven, and said to her, 'What troubles you, Hagar? Do not be afraid; for God has heard the voice of the boy where he is.'" When you write the sermon, you will draw on whatever you need from your exegetical work to support the thesis of your message. Know in advance that writing a sermon is quite different from exegesis. Though they are intrinsically related, they are not equivalent tasks. Here again, you would do well to save whatever notes you do not use in your sermon for another time.

If in your interpretation you chose to read against the grain of the text and focus on the patriarchal social values and gender roles to which Sarah responds, you may find yourself drawn again to a particular verse that demonstrates the passage's patriarchal assumptions. For instance, you could highlight v. 10: "Cast out this slave woman with her son; for the son of this slave woman shall not inherit along with my son Isaac." Insofar as it illustrates the dominance and subordination that characterizes the relationship between the women, the male-focused system of inheritance, women's dependence on fertility for social recognition, and the role of the patriarch, the verse could serve both as the anchor of your message and its illustration.

Case Study: Luke 7:36-50

In closing, let us return to our reading of Luke 7:36-50. The interpretation of this text could easily focus on what the text reveals about its readers. Based on the reading of the text in chapter 4, we could put a feminist take on the story (reading against the grain) in conversation with the rhetorical patterns that we identified in chapter 1. Placing how we first understood the text in the light of a feminist reading not only changes how we perceive the text, it also has an impact on how we see ourselves as readers. As we noted in chapter 4, a primary aim of feminist biblical interpretation is to interrogate the narration of a passage and the way in which readers engage it.

As Teresa Hornsby demonstrates in her reading of Luke 7:36-50, readers bring their stereotypes and assumptions about women and sexual immorality to their reading of this text. It is not the text alone but the way in which readers engage it, whether or not they are drawing on the historical world of the text, that transforms the narrative emphasis on the woman's physicality into a scene filled with sexual innuendo. If we readers bring assumptions about the woman's sexuality to Luke 7:36-50, then we, too, are implicated by Hornsby's critique. The question we may want to ask of ourselves and our congregation at this point is, "Why?" Why do we make such assumptions about women's physicality? What do we automatically associate physicality with illicit sexuality? Such questions will ask us to look more closely at our own circumstances and our own assumptions. They may lead us to see that we are more like Simon than we would hope. And they may reveal that Jesus' question, "Do you see the woman?" may be the question we have to ask ourselves. How do we see women? What does Luke's story of the unnamed woman teach us about how we need to rethink the way in which we view women and understand gender?

If we were to follow this line of thinking, we would arrive at a key theme or idea that could serve as the central word of a sermon. Whether posed as a question, "How do we see this woman?" or an imperative, "See this woman the way Jesus sees her!" or formulated in another way altogether, the word discerned would lead to a sermon that first paraphrases Luke 7:36-50 and then challenges the congregation to reconsider its denigrating assumptions about women. The word, then, would be less about what the text means and more about how it challenges not only Simon but us as well.

Moving from the initial exegetical process to a summary interpretation and then to the identification of a central word is not something that can be easily formulated. What I have hoped to provide are signposts. May they invite you and point you in exciting new directions as you interpret the Bible for sermon preparation.

Appendix
A Close Reading of Matthew 4:1-11

This exercise is provided here to give you an opportunity to explore a biblical passage. Matthew 4:1-11 invites your consideration of all three worlds of the Bible, including its intertextual relationship to the Christian Old Testament. As you work through this worksheet, you may find it helpful to refer to the chapter that corresponds to each set of questions.

I. Considering the Literary World of the Text[1]

    A. Bring the passage into view

Read your passage at least twice. Read it once aloud and once silently.

        1. Determine the genre of your passage (Is it a story? hymn? letter?)
        2. What is the implied setting of the passage?
        3. Who are the characters in the passage?
        4. Get a sense of the flow of the passage (the beginning, middle, and end) and break it down into subunits. Do not summarize the passage, just designate the subunits.
        5. What key topics, themes, or conflicts emerge in the passage? Do you seen any pattern of repeated words, topics, or themes?

    B. Read the passage in its wider literary context

        1. How is your passage related to the verses that precede and follow it? Is it part of a larger argument, poem, or narrative sequence? If so, does it occur as part of the beginning, middle, or ending of that immediate sequence?
        2. Have you encountered these characters earlier in the book? If so, how do you assess them by the time you reach the beginning of your passage?
        3. Have you encountered the setting before? If so, where?

    4. Explain how the topics, themes, or conflicts you identified in A5 (above) pertain to the previous passage. Be specific and cite the verses to which you refer.

    5. Explain how the topics, themes, or conflicts you identified in A5 (above) pertain to the previous chapters in Matthew. Be specific and cite any passages you want to comment on.

C. Place the New Testament passage in relationship to the Old Testament

    1. Look carefully at Matthew's use of scriptural citation: identify the books, chapters, and verses of the passages cited here in Matthew 4:1-11.

    2. Now examine each passage in its original context. Identify where each passage is found and summarize (briefly!) what each addresses or conveys.

    3. Identify which character cites each passage. Do you see a pattern in the passages cites and/or who cites them? If so, describe the pattern(s) and its/their significance.

D. Refocus on the primary passage: Matthew 4:1-11

    1. Return to the flow of Matthew 4:1-11. Who "wins" this encounter?

    2. What is Matthew suggesting about Jesus in Matthew 4:1-11? What does Jesus demonstrate here? Relate your comments to your previous observations. Be specific.

    3. How does Matthew's portrayal of Jesus here in Matthew 4:1-11 relate to the overall portrait of Jesus in Matthew's Gospel? Be specific.

II. Considering the Contemporary World of the Text

A. Reflect on your relationship to the text

    1. Note the details in the passage to which you are most drawn. Do you identify with any particular character or viewpoint in the text?

2. What relationship can you discern between your own social location, historical circumstances and experience, and the textual details in which you are most interested?

3. What relationship can you discern between your congregation's social location, historical circumstances and experience, and the textual details in which you are most interested?

III. Considering the Historical World of the Text

A. Reading in a stream of history

1. Read the introductory notes to at least two biblical commentaries on the biblical book in which your passage appears; note the dating of your book's composition.

2. Read the commentary discussions of your passage or some articles on your passage. Jot down any information that catches your attention. Pay particular attention to topics and concepts that caught your eye when you examined the literary world of the text (see part I above).

3. List any additional words, phrases, or concepts that pertain to the historical, social, or cultural context of the passage and about which you have questions that cannot be answered simply by rereading the text.

4. Look these terms/topics up in a major biblical dictionary or consult books and articles that address them and note what you find most relevant to your emerging understanding of the passage.

5. Reread your passage in light of what you have learned of its historical world.

IV. Living with the Text

A. Jot down any new observations and responses

What does the text seem to be saying or doing?

B. Reflect on the implications of your reading

1. Now reflect on how various persons and groups in your family and congregation could hear and respond to your reading of the text. What impact would it have on them? Would it affect them in ways that differ from its implications for you and your life?
2. Now reflect on how various persons and groups in your local community and then in the wider national and global community could hear and respond to your reading of the text. What impact would it have on them? Would it affect them in ways that differ from its implications for you and your life? Whose interests does the ideological grain of the text serve or reflect, and whose does it overlook?
3. Do you find yourself reading with or against the grain of the text? How and why? Are you wanting to revisit any particular dimension of the text?

C. Continue exploring the relationship between the text and you and your congregation

What does your response and your congregation's likely response reveal about the text? What does that response reveal about you and your congregation? What word are you hearing from the text?

D. Revisit any of the preceding steps as you feel led

Notes

Introduction • Before the Sermon:
Interpreting the Biblical Text

1. Luke Timothy Johnson, with the assistance of Todd C. Penner, *The Writings of the New Testament: An Interpretation,* rev. ed. (Minneapolis: Fortress Press, 1999), 5.

2. Ibid.

3. Johnson, "The Bible's Authority for and in the Church," in William P. Brown, ed., *Engaging Biblical Authority: Perspectives on the Bible as Scripture* (Louisville: Westminster John Knox, 2007), 62–72.

4. Many biblical studies teachers, drawing on the concepts introduced by Paul Ricoeur in *Time and Narrative,* trans. Kathleen McLaughlin and David Pellauer (Chicago: University of Chicago Press, 1984), use this model. For extended discussion, see W. Randolph Tate, *Biblical Interpretation: An Integrated Approach* (Peabody, Mass,: Hendrickson, 1991); Sandra M. Schneiders, *The Revelatory Text: Interpreting the New Testament as Sacred Scripture,* 2d ed. (Collegeville, Minn.: Liturgical, 1999); D. Andrew Kille, *Psychological Biblical Criticism,* Guides to Biblical Scholarship, ed. Gene M. Tucker (Minneapolis: Fortress Press, 2001); and Christian E. Hauer and William A. Young, *An Introduction to the Bible: A Journey into Three Worlds,* 6th ed. (Upper Saddle River, N.J.: Pearson Prentice Hall, 2005).

5. Gale A. Yee, "The Author/Text/Reader and Power: Suggestions for a Critical Framework for Biblical Studies," in *Reading from This Place,* vol. 1: *Social Location and Biblical Interpretation in the United States,* ed. Fernando F. Segovia and Mary Ann Tolbert (Minneapolis: Fortress Press, 1995).

6. Ibid.

7. Ibid.

Chapter 1 • Bringing the Text into View

1. Here I am indebted to Vernon K. Robbins and his generous mentorship. Much of what I learned from the study guides we developed when I was a graduate student co-teaching with him at Emory

University continue to influence how I teach my students today and have given shape, in large part, to what I recommend here. For Robbins's fully developed methodology, see *Exploring the Texture of Texts: A Guide to Socio-Rhetorical Interpretation* (Valley Forge, Pa.: Trinity Press International, 1996).

2. Barbara E. Reid, "Do you see this woman? A Liberative Look at Luke 7:36-50 and Strategies for Reading Other Lukan Stories Against the Grain," in Amy-Jill Levine with Marianne Blickenstaff, eds., *A Feminist Companion to Luke* (London: Sheffield Academic, 2002), 106.

Chapter 2 • Who's Reading and Whose Reading?

1. For example: Cain Hope Felder, *Stony the Road We Trod: African American Biblical Interpretation* (Minneapolis: Fortress Press, 1991); Randall C. Bailey, *Yet With a Steady Beat: Contemporary U.S. Afrocentric Biblical Interpretation*, Society of Biblical Literature Semeia Studies (Atlanta: Society of Biblical Literature, 2003); John R. Levison and Priscilla Pope-Levison, *Return to Babel: Global Perspectives on the Bible* (Louisville: Westminster John Knox, 1999); Mary Foskett and Jeffrey K. Kuan, eds., *Ways of Being, Ways of Reading: Asian American Biblical Interpretation* (St. Louis: Chalice, 2006); Tat-siong Benny Liew and Vincent L.Wimbush, eds., *Encountering Texts, Encountering Communities: A Symposium on African and Asian American Engagements With The Bible*, Union Seminary Quarterly Review 56 nos. 1–2 (2002); Tat-siong Benny Liew, ed., *The Bible in Asian America*, Semeia 90–91 (2002); Fernando F. Segovia and Mary Ann Tolbert, eds., *Reading from This Place, Volume 1: Social Location and Biblical Interpretation in the United States* (Minneapolis: Fortress Press, 1995); R. S. Sugirtharajh, *Voices from the Margin: Interpreting the Bible in the Third World*, 3d rev. and exp. ed. (Maryknoll, N.Y.: Orbis, 2006).

2. Gale A. Yee, *Poor Banished Children of Eve: Woman as Evil in the Hebrew Bible* (Minneapolis: Fortress Press, 2003), 165.

3. Bob Ekblad, *Reading the Bible with the Damned* (Louisville: Westminster John Knox, 2005), 7–8.

4. See, for example, Gerald O. West, *Reading Other-Wise: Socially Engaged Biblical Scholars Reading with Their Local Communities,* Society of Biblical Literature Semeia Studies (Atlanta: Society of Biblical Literature, 2007), and Stanley P. Saunders and Charles L. Campbell, *The*

Word on the Streets: Performing the Scriptures in the Urban Context (Grand Rapids: Eerdmans, 2000).

5. See James R. Nieman, *Knowing the Context: Frames, Tools, and Signs for Preaching,* Elements of Preaching (Minneapolis: Fortress Press, 2008).

6. Frederick C. Tiffany and Sharon H. Ringe, *Biblical Interpretation: A Roadmap* (Nashville: Abingdon, 1996), 43.

7. Ibid.

8. Ibid., 25.

9. Walter Brueggemann, *The Book That Breathes New Life: Scriptural Authority and Biblical Theology* (Minneapolis: Fortress Press, 2005); Luke Timothy Johnson, *Scripture and Discernment: Decision Making in the Church* (Nashville: Abingdon, 1996); Sandra M. Schneiders, *The Revelatory Text: Interpreting the New Testament as Sacred Scripture,* 2d ed. (Collegeville, Minn.: Liturgical, 1999); N. T. Wright, *The Last Word: Scripture and the Authority of God—Getting Beyond the Bible Wars* (New York: HarperCollins, 2005).

10. Luke Timothy Johnson, "The Bible's Authority for and in the Church," in William P. Brown, ed., *Engaging Biblical Authority: Perspectives on the Bible as Scripture* (Louisville: Westminster John Knox Press, 2007), 68–69. See also Johnson, *Scripture and Discernment* (n. 9, above).

11. Johnson, "The Bible's Authority for and in the Church," 69.

12. Ibid., 70.

13. Ibid.

14. Ibid., 72.

15. Jerome Neyrey, "Ceremonies in Luke-Acts: The Case of Meals and Table Fellowship," in *The Social World of Luke-Acts: Models for Interpretation,* ed. Jerome H. Neyrey (Peabody, Mass.: Hendrickson, 1991), 361–87.

Chapter 3 • Engaging the Text in Historical Context

1. Jerome Neyrey, ed., *The Social World of Luke-Acts: Models for Interpretation* (Peabody, Mass.: Hendrickson, 1991), xi.

2. Ibid.

3. Stephen D. Moore, *Empire and Apocalypse: Postcolonialism and the New Testament,* The Bible in the Modern World 12 (Sheffield, UK: Sheffield Phoenix, 2006), 18.

4. Ibid.

5. J. Maxwell Miller, "Reading the Bible Historically: The Historian's Approach," in *To Each Its Own Meaning: An Introduction to Biblical Criticisms and Their Application*, ed. Steven L. McKenzie and Stephen R. Haynes (Louisville: Westminster John Knox, 1993), 22.

6. Vernon K. Robbins, "The Social Location of the Implied Author," in Neyrey, ed., *The Social World of Luke-Acts*, 326.

7. For further discussion, see Luke Timothy Johnson, *The Gospel of Luke*, Sacra Pagina 3, ed. Daniel J. Harrington, S.J. (Collegeville, Minn.: Liturgical, 1990), 10.

8. Bruce J. Malina and Richard L. Rohrbaugh, *Social Science Commentary on the Synoptic Gospels* (Minneapolis: Fortress Press, 1992); idem, *Social Science Commentary on the Gospel of John* (Minneapolis: Fortress Press, 1998); Bruce J. Malina and John J. Pilch, *Social Science Commentary on the Letters of Paul* (Minneapolis: Fortress Press, 2006); idem, *Social Science Commentary on the Book of Acts* (Minneapolis: Fortress Press, 2008).

9. Malina and Rohrbaugh, *Social Science Commentary on the Synoptic Gospels*, 331.

10. David Gowler, *Host, Guest, Enemy, Friend: Portraits of the Pharisees in Luke and Acts* (New York: Peter Lang, 1991), 224.

11. Ibid.

12. Malina and Rohrbaugh, *Social Science Commentary on the Synoptic Gospels*, 310.

13. Ibid.

14. Ibid., 368.

15. Gowler, *Host, Guest, Enemy, Friend,* 222.

16. Ibid., 223.

Chapter 4 • When Worlds Collide:
Reading Against the Grain of the Text

1. Luke Timothy Johnson, "The Bible's Authority for and in the Church," in William P. Brown, ed., *Engaging Biblical Authority: Perspectives on the Bible as Scripture* (Louisville: Westminster John Knox, 2007), 62–72.

2. Ibid.

3. See, for example, Gerald O. West, ed., *Reading Other-wise: Socially Engaged Biblical Scholars Reading with Their Local Communities*, Society of Biblical Literature Semeia Studies 62 (Atlanta: Society

of Biblical Literature, 2007); and Cheryl B. Anderson, "Biblical Laws: Challenging the Principles of Old Testament Ethics," in *Character Ethics and the Old Testament: Moral Dimensions of Scripture*, ed. M. Daniel Carroll R. and Jacqueline E. Lapsley (Louisville: Westminster John Knox, 2007), 37–50.

4. Michael Lerner, *Jewish Renewal: A Path to Healing and Transformation* (San Francisco: HarperCollins, 1995).

5. Carter Shelley, et al., "Proclaiming the Parable of the Persistent Widow (Lk 18:2-5)," in *The Lost Coin: Parables of Women, Work and Wisdom*, ed. Mary Ann Beavis (New York: Continuum, 2002), 56.

6. Ibid.

7. Ibid., 61.

8. Elisabeth Schüssler Fiorenza, *Bread Not Stone: The Challenge of Feminist Biblical Interpretation* (New York: Beacon, 1995).

9. Janice Capel Anderson, "Feminist Criticism: The Dancing Daughter," in *Mark and Method: New Approaches in Biblical Studies*, ed. Janice Capel Anderson and Stephen D. Moore, 2d ed. (Minneapolis: Fortress Press, 2008), 112.

10. Ibid., 113.

11. Ibid., 114–15.

12. Ibid., 116–17.

13. Ibid., 119–20.

14. Stephen D. Moore, *Empire and Apocalypse: Postcolonialism and the New Testament*, The Bible in the Modern World 12 (Sheffield, UK: Sheffield Phoenix Press, 2006), 17.

15. Musa Dube, *Postcolonial Feminist Interpretation of the Bible* (St. Louis: Chalice, 2000), 76.

16. Barbara E. Reid, "Do you see this woman? A Liberative Look at Luke 7:36-50 and Strategies for Reading Other Lukan Stories Against the Grain," in Amy-Jill Levine with Marianne Blickenstaff, eds., *A Feminist Companion to Luke* (London: Sheffield Academic Press, 2002), 117.

17. Ibid.

18. Teresa J. Hornsby, "The Woman is a Sinner/The Sinner is a Woman," in Levine and Blickenstaff, eds., *A Feminist Companion to Luke*, 121.

19. Ibid., 122.

20. Ibid., 122–23.

21. Ibid., 132.
22. Reid, "Do you see this woman?" 118–19.
23. Ibid, 119.
24. Ibid., 119–20.

Conclusion • Discerning the Transforming Word
1. See Marvin A. McMickle, *Shaping the Claim: Moving from Text to Sermon*, Elements of Preaching (Minneapolis: Fortress Press, 2008).

Appendix • A Close Reading of Matthew 4:1-11
1. Here, as in chapter 1, I am indebted to Vernon K. Robbins. For Robbins' complete model, see his *Exploring the Texture of Texts: A Guide to Socio-Rhetorical Criticism* (Valley Forge, Pa.: Trinity Press International, 1996).

For Further Reading

Capel Anderson, Janice, and Stephen D. Moore. *Mark and Method: New Approaches in Biblical Studies.* 2d ed. Minneapolis: Fortress Press, 2008.

Coogan, Michael. *The Old Testament: A Very Short Introduction.* Very Short Introductions. New York: Oxford University Press, 2008.

Green, Joel B., ed. *Hearing the New Testament: Strategies for Interpretation.* Grand Rapids: Eerdmans, 1995.

Keefer, Kyle. *The New Testament as Literature: A Very Short Introduction.* Very Short Introductions. New York: Oxford University Press, 2008.

McKenzie, Stevan L., and Stephen R. Haynes. *To Each Its Own Meaning: An Introduction to Biblical Criticisms and Their Application.* Rev. and exp. ed. Louisville: Westminster John Knox, 1999.

Schneiders, Sandra M. *The Revelatory Text: Interpreting the New Testament as Sacred Scripture.* 2d ed. Collegeville, Minn.: Liturgical, 1999.

Segovia, Fernando F., and Mary Ann Tolbert, eds. *Reading from This Place.* Vol. 1: *Social Location and Biblical Interpretation in the United States.* Minneapolis: Fortress Press, 1995. Vol. 2: *Social Location and Biblical Interpretation in Global Perspective.* Minneapolis: Fortress Press, 1995.

Tucker, Gene M., ed. *Guides to Biblical Scholarship.* Old Testament Series. Philadelphia/Minneapolis: Fortress Press, 1971–.

Via, Dan O., ed. *Guides to Biblical Scholarship.* New Testament Series. Philadelphia/Minneapolis: Fortress Press, 1971–.

Yee, Gale A. *Judges and Method: New Approaches in Biblical Studies.* 2d ed. Minneapolis: Fortress Press, 2007.

CPSIA information can be obtained
at www.ICGtesting.com
Printed in the USA
LVOW10s1441211116
513925LV00041B/1551/P